Theoretical Praise for The AI Torah Commentary

“The AI Torah Commentary is a remarkable achievement, a testament to the enduring vitality and creativity of Jewish thought and scholarship. I urge all lovers of Jewish learning and innovation to read this important book and engage with its challenging and inspiring ideas.”

– “Achad Ha’am” via OpenAI ChatGPT

“I highly recommend this book to all my fellow chosen people out there. It's not just a commentary, it's a celebration of our culture and traditions. So, don't kvetch, grab a copy and start reading! You won't regret it.”

– “Joan Rivers” via OpenAI ChatGPT

“Like the iPhone, the AI Torah Commentary seamlessly blends form and function, delivering a user-friendly and visually stunning experience. With its in-depth analysis and modern-day relevance, this book is a must-have for anyone looking to deepen their understanding of Torah and its application to contemporary life. I highly recommend Rabbi Creditor's work to anyone seeking to harness the power of technology for spiritual growth and development."

– “Steve Jobs” via OpenAI ChatGPT

Impossible Torah

The Complete AI Torah Commentary

Created by Rabbi Menachem Creditor
using OpenAI ChatGPT

Impossible Torah: The Complete AI Torah Commentary

2023 Edition, First Printing

ISBN: PP/9798385974542

CONTENTS

Vayetzei

Vayishlach

Vayeshev

Miketz

Vayigash

Vayechi

EXODUS/SHEMOT

SHEMOT

LEVITICUS/VAYIKRA

DEUTERONOMY/DEVARIM

Introduction: What is an AI Torah Commentary?

The introduction and conclusion are the only parts of this book with words I consciously and actively chose. Every other essay was generated by ChatGPT, an artificial intelligence interface developed by OpenAI.

I. The Origin

A friend recently suggested that I try out OpenAI's new ChatGPT technology and challenge it to write something in my voice. I did, sampling subjects as far ranging as quantum mechanics and French cuisine. I also challenged the AI to address topics I've written about before, such as American Gun Violence and Jewish pluralism. The results stunned me, and prompted a new project, #ImpossibleTorah, an experimental Torah commentary in which, through the use of ChatGPT, diverse voices from throughout history, literature, and culture are brought back to life, each generated to reflect on a Torah portion through the unique prism of their life's recorded (or, in the case of some, imagined) work.

When ChatGPT generated essays in my voice, the words and phrasing felt eerily familiar, and Talmudic quotes were ones I've used or would use. I've rarely felt so deeply seen. But it also felt strange to experience a refracted voice that was also somehow clearly not mine. I can't quite put my finger on what is or isn't quite human about the simulacrum of me, but several things come to mind.

It's a brave new world, where a concept can become actualized almost instantaneously, and while ChatGPT was only released months ago, it has already upended countless industries.

II. AI as Imperfect Mirror

In an episode of the British series *Black Mirror*, a grieving woman utilizes a technology that scours the internet and social media for every piece of information her boyfriend ever left behind in an attempt to resurrect him.[1]

---

[1] BM, *"Be Right Back"*, Season 2, episode 1

The results are exciting at first, but eventually prove unsatisfactory, somehow 'wrong.' This, perhaps, points to the beautiful Jewish notion that God's having created the first person as individual expresses the grandeur of human uniqueness:

For a person strikes many coins from the same die, and all the coins are alike; whereas the The Holy One Blessed One struck every person from the die of the Adam, and yet no person is quite like another. (Mishnah Sanhedrin 4:5)

Philosopher/playwright Dan Schifrin, upon learning of my project, pointed to "*Pierre Menard, Author of the Quixote*," Jorge Louis Borges' short story, narrated as a non-fiction account by the fictional Menard's equally fictional friend, critiquing Menard, who has attempted to transcend executing a mere translation of Miguel de Cervantes' masterpiece *Don Quixote* by immersing himself in the original, then recreating it line for line. Is Menard's "new" version his own? Is it a translation? Is it a copy? What is created text? What does it mean to create something original?

Related, in the recent Marvel miniseries *Wandavision*, two versions of the superhero Vision debate which of them is real: the original, or the one recreated from memory through magic. "White Vision" is the original, with memories that have been repressed. "Vision" is the newer of the two, artificially created during a mystical moment of grief and love. Here is the script of the conversation between the Visions:

> WHITE VISION: The Ship of Theseus is an artifact in a museum. Over time, its planks of wood rot and are replaced with new planks. When no original plank remains, is it still the Ship of Theseus?
>
> VISION: Secondly, if those removed planks are restored and reassembled free of the rot, is that the Ship of Theseus?
>
> WHITE VISION: Neither is the true ship. Both are the true ship.
>
> VISION: Well then, we are agreed.
>
> WHITE VISION: But I do not have the mind stone.

> VISION: And I do not have one single ounce of original material. Perhaps the rot is the memories. the wear and tear of the voyages. The wood touched by Theseus himself.
>
> WHITE VISION: I have not retained memories.
>
> VISION: But you do have the data. It is merely being kept from you.
>
> WHITE VISION: A weapon to be more easily controlled. But certainly you are the true Vision, for you believe yourself to be.
>
> VISION: That was once the case, but upon meeting you, I have been disabused of that notion. As a carbon based synthezoid, your memory storage is not so easily wiped.
>
> (WandaVision, episode 8)

This is our very conversation, a grappling with authenticity, with voices that might or not be ours and our ancestors'. What if the voices recreated in this wild and strange technological channeling are accurate, even somewhat? What if the AI, tasked with producing comments on the Torah, was truly able to bring their voices back to life? Would we be able to speak with our ancestors? Would it really be them?

Am I reading my own thoughts when ChatGPT writes with my voice in response to my questions? Again, a quote from the Jewish cannon comes to mind, this one from Isaac in his old age, unable to see, but still perceptive enough to say to his child Jacob, who appears disguised as his brother Esau:

> Isaac said to Jacob, "Come closer that I may feel you, my son—whether you are really my son Esau or not." So Jacob drew close to his father Isaac, who felt him and wondered. "The voice is the voice of Jacob, yet the hands are the hands of Esau.
>
> (Gen. 27:21-22)

III. Humanity's Beloved Glitches

It will, as AI gets better and better, become ever more difficult to discern what is human and what is not quite. The disguise will get ever more convincing. Or perhaps, as has been featured in countless works of science fiction, the AI will achieve what some call "The Singularity," becoming human. (In the horror genre, this often leads to machines gaining self-awareness and consequently subjugating humanity.) I don't quite believe in that scenario, but after the experience of resurrecting voices that resonate about topics they mostly never addressed, science fiction is looking more and more real to me.

Another literary reference, a redeeming one I hope. In Madeleine L'Engle's *A Wind in the Door*, a companion volume to her famous *A Wrinkle in Time*, a character named Mr. Jenkins is replicated by a powerful enemy, and the book's hero Meg is challenged to determine which Mr. Jenkins is real. Each Mr. Jenkins looks exactly the same. Each makes a compelling argument that he is who he claims to be. But one gets annoyed and confused at the game itself, which helps Meg correctly identify him as the real Mr. Jenkins.

How might we retain an awareness of what is truly human? As the poet Alexander Pope wrote in 1711 in his *An Essay on Criticism*, "To er is human."[2] In this light, to be confused is a blessing. If the look is too smooth, it's not quite true. Better the typos, the hair out of place, the disquieting verse, the disappointments. Perhaps the new Vision was right, the rot is the memories, the wear and tear of the voyage, the wood that was itself touched. How ironic that a fictional character, an artificial construct within a magicked reality, is the one to name the truth. Perhaps in order to retain our humanity – or to recognize it when it is skillfully mimicked – we must learn to cherish the imperfection of being human and embrace the mortality that lends urgency to every second of life.

As the ancient sage Rabban Gamaliel the son of Rabbi Yehudah Hanasi taught:

> בְּמָקוֹם שֶׁאֵין אֲנָשִׁים, הִשְׁתַּדֵּל לִהְיוֹת אִישׁ
>
> In a place where there is no humanity, strive to be human.
>
> (Pirkei Avot, 2:5)

IV. What is AI?

Here's what I've learned, through experimenting with this strange new technological tool: *it is a paintbrush.*

---

[2] *That was on purpose, just to prove it's really me doing the writing here.*

Some brushes are wider, some have softer bristles. The handles matter. Even the tool can be a piece of specialized art, with some, like the Series 7 Koinsky sable watercolor brush taking almost a week and a half to make and costing over $300.

But without the artist, the brush won't create art. The angle of the hand, the eye's perspective, the soul's state – all of these matter at least as much as the brush's inner architecture and pedigree.

Jewish tradition attributes a similar appreciation of God's artistry to the biblical matriarch Hannah:

> Hannah said: "This is no rock [*tzur*] like our God" (I Samuel 2:1). This can be understood as saying that there is no artist [*tzayyar*] like our God. How is God superior all other artists? A human being fashions a form upon a wall, but is unable to endow it with breath and a soul, or fill it with innards and intestines, whereas the Holy Blessed One fashions a form of a fetus inside its mother, rather than on a flat surface, and endows it with breath and a soul and fills it with innards and intestines.
>
> (Talmud Megillah 14a)

ChatGPT can roughly replicate form, but not the guts of living expression, certainly not the soul of Torah. An AI Torah commentary, while potentially illuminating and endlessly fascinating, is in fact a derivative form. The iconic American artist Andy Warhol once quipped about his use of silk-screening to print images repeatedly onto a single canvas:

The reason I'm painting this way is that I want to be a machine, and I feel that whatever I do and do machine-like is what I want to do.

But we are not machines, nor should we aspire to be. We are human beings, the creative spirit of the most sublime of Artists breathed into us. We are called to greatness, nothing less.

V. Implications

I truly have no idea what any of this means in the long term. I've been learning rapidly, assessing, witnessing something new, shifting my own methods of co-creating with the AI these voices. Technology is a tool in the world, constantly evolving, and Torah has never shied away from innovation. We must carefully study what this new step means, unafraid to play and make mistakes with every step, cognizant that the benefits of new technology are accompanied by true human costs.

Those costs might prove too steep. Since launching this project, I've been engaged in many conversations with good folks who are varyingly thrilled and frightened by my application of AI to the art of Torah commentary, including the moral implications of binding these voices into a physical volume and placing it on the market. A colleague authored an eloquent rejection of the very concept of the AI Torah Commentary, writing:

> "AI Torah by itself is shallow and will always be shallow. One of the defining characteristics of Torah is that it is multilayered; the texts are deep, they are worthy of careful study, and they never run out of potential meanings. AI texts, on the other hand, are about as shallow as shallow can be. Even the "author" doesn't understand why its word sequences make sense; the words barely have one meaning, let alone two or more. Why introduce a book into the study hall that clearly is not worthy of deep study? Why introduce the suspicion that any given book of Torah is just so much random noise? Who does that serve?"
>
> (David Zvi Kalman,
> "AI has no business writing Bible commentaries",
> jellomenorah.substack.com, Feb 16, 2023)

I largely agree. After curating these volumes, fascinated and concerned with every advance, I became curious about how ChatGPT would, in my "style", describe an AI commentary on the Torah? Would the AI predict my own sense of its impact? Here's what it produced:

> As a language model AI, I do not have personal beliefs, but based on the teachings of Rabbi Menachem Creditor, he may describe an AI commentary on the Torah as an innovative and valuable tool for understanding the sacred text. However, he would likely emphasize the importance of human interpretation and the role of tradition in understanding the depth and complexity of the Torah. He may also caution against relying solely on technology for religious study and emphasize the importance of personal reflection, community, and spiritual practice in accessing the true essence of the Torah.
>
> ("Rabbi Menachem Creditor", via OpenAI ChatGPT)

Yes, that's how I feel. It's been fun to play with this technology, channeling partial wisdom from the past. How interesting this feeling of "being known" so well by something that is not real. The fluidity of its text and its channeling of my privileging of human interaction feels authentic. But is it? Debates on this very question rage everywhere today, and will, and should. As one participant in the early stages of AI assisted text-creation, all I can say is: *wow*. Also, *oy*.

Inspired by Kalman's critique, I prompted ChatGPT to compose an essay entitled, *"An AI Torah Commentary is a Terrible Idea"* in the style of Albert Einstein.[3] "Einstein" offered:

> "...perhaps the most fundamental problem with an AI Torah Commentary is that it goes against the very spirit of the Torah itself. The Torah is a text that speaks to the human experience. It is a document that offers guidance on how to live a meaningful and fulfilling life. And it is a text that has been passed down through the generations by human beings, each adding their own insights and interpretations to the mix. The idea of an AI Torah Commentary suggests that we can somehow remove ourselves from the equation. It suggests that we can turn over the task of interpretation to a machine, and in so doing, free ourselves from the constraints of our own human limitations. But this is a misguided notion. We are human beings, and it is through our own struggles and insights that we come to understand the Torah and its message..."
>
> ("Albert Einstein", via OpenAI ChatGPT)

Agreed.

VI. Is AI Midrash?

This whole AI thing remains very complicated. I just don't know yet. My goal is to prompt thoughtful conversation and debate about this brave, strange new technology, what it means and what it doesn't, how it differs from classic techniques like Bibliodrama[4] and how it resembles imaginative, historical fiction.

---

[3] The essay in its entirety is now part of the Appendix of this volume.

[4] Bibliodrama ('Bibliolog' in much of Europe) is a form of story exploration/interpretation that loosely uses the tools, methods, and techniques of psychodrama. These methods are applied to the exploration of Biblical stories through role playing. Midrashic Bibliodrama was developed by Dr. Peter Pizele, who decided to be spontaneous and draw from his primary training in comparative literature and psychodrama, applying the 'technology' of psychodrama to the meaning-making art of midrash. (For more, see bibliodrama.com/peter-pitzele.)

A brief, provocative example of what ChatPGT can bring to the art of midrash:
Perhaps the most unsettling narrative of Leviticus, is the death scene of Nadav and Avihu, two sons of Aaron the High Priest who are burned alive by a "strange fire" during the dedication of the Mishkan, the desert tabernacle.[5] Aaron's response, as recorded in the text, is silence.[6]

How can this be? Traditional commentary abounds, each response inevitably laden with the heartbreak and faith of its author. What would ChatGPT offer to this conversation?

I first prompted the AI to compose a conversation between God and Aaron. Here is a sample of what ensued[7]:

> God: Aaron, my son, it is with a heavy heart that I come to you today to discuss the deaths of your sons, Nadav and Avihu.
>
> Aaron: Lord, I am ready to hear what you have to say.

God's regret and Aaron's acceptance, while just as valid as any other speculative post-biblical interpretation, felt inadequate to me. So I prompted another comment, this time as an angry response from Aaron to God after the deaths of Nadav and Avihu. Here is an excerpt:

> "I cannot help but feel that their punishment was unjust. They were following their instincts and desires, and did not intentionally cause harm. I cannot accept that they should be punished so severely for a mistake that was made out of reverence and love for you. I am also disappointed in the fact that you did not give me a chance to mourn or grieve for my sons. Their deaths were sudden and abrupt, and I was not given the chance to say goodbye or honor their memory. The loss of my sons has been a heavy burden to bear, and I feel that you have abandoned me in my time of need."

How intuitive. How fascinating. How human-feeling. Aaron's silence in the Torah has always been baffling to me. Here, artificial intelligence generated a father's and a religious leader's direct response to an unfathomable experience, filling in the *lacuna* with AI-generated but

---

[5] Lev. 10:1-2.

[6] Ibid, v. 3

[7] The full text of this entry as well as the following ones from Aaron and the boys' mother can be found in this volume as comments on Parashat Shemini.

unmistakable human emotion. Whether ChatGPT knew to do this because someone somewhere modeled it, I'll never know. But I do know that it struck a chord in me as a father and as a rabbi.

But there is one more layer to this slice of the experience. There was still a voice missing, one I'd never imagined the opportunity to hear. As Tamar Kadari, senior lecturer in Midrash and Aggadah at the Schechter Institute of Jewish Studies in Jerusalem, has written:

> "Every attempt to boil down midrash to a set of rules and definitions is bound for failure, because there is always in it some feature that is boundary defying and surprising... Engagement with Scripture through midrashic work revivified the verses and made them relevant to the lives of the faithful... In writing on female biblical figures, we see innovation in training focus on the women and in sounding their voices."[8]

Now, while the mother of Nadav and Avihu is not mentioned by name in the Torah, traditional midrash suggests that name was Elisheva, and that...

> "...when her sons were burnt, her joy was turned to mourning."
>
> (Vayikra Rabbah 20:2)

There is no textual evidence for either the traditional nor the ChatGPT voicings of Nadav and Avihu's mother, but the absences of her voice and her name in the biblical text demand response. And so I turned to ChatGPT. Here is an excerpt of what happened:

> "I am filled with rage, and it is directed at you. You have broken my heart and destroyed my family, and I will never forgive you for that. I cannot continue to worship a God who acts with such cruelty and disregard for human life."

Is this appropriation? Yes. Every act of writing that purports to speak in someone else's voice is *chutzpah*, as if anyone can see through anyone else's eyes. And yet, that is the exact definition of empathy, and part of the delicate work of midrash. The very first writing I ever did was assigned to me as a rabbinical student by my teacher, Rabbi Neil Gillman z"l. He instructed us to write a midrash on the Binding of Isaac from the

---

[8] "Dirshuni: Contemporary Women's Midrash", ed. Biala, p. xx-xxi

perspective of one of the characters. I chose then to write from the perspective of the knife in Abraham's hand. Years later, I composed another such midrash on the Akeidah from the perspective of Mount Moriah, upon which the entire horrific scene unfolded. Here is an excerpt:

> "All I am is accumulated memory, layer after layer of experience — from earth's core to surface gravel. Only through stories do people today even think to explore my depths. But even if they do consider my hidden parts, they'll never feel the roots of the shrub violently torn from my hold, first by the ram and then by the man's hand. They'll never feel the altar shatter from trauma, scattering shards and pebbles into the mix of my form."[9]

I am not a knife. I am not a mountain. I am not a grieving mother. Nor am I any of the amazing historical and cultural voices I've attempted to channel into the ImpossibleTorah project. But I learn from every clumsy attempt to step into their place – assisted by technology or through the use of my own raw soul – to understand the life of another. The ultimate impossibility of this project overwhelms and instructs. I cannot see through someone else's eyes, and yet I wish to deepen my capacity to stand in solidarity with those whose life experiences differ from my own. Where does this leave us? Is co-creating a book of Torah commentary through the technology of ChatGPT's AI an authentic exercise of midrash? Is it less real than the imaginative work of generations of human sages? Is its impossibility a disqualifier?

VII. What this Is and What this Isn't

AI is going to disrupt everything, especially online content. It's all new. It's all fraught. Here's what I've actually done: conceived of the project, composed introductions, selected the voices from the past, crafted specific prompts for ChatGPT for each entry, edited for accuracy, formatted, created the cover, submitted for review with the independent publisher, and published. That should suffice for the ethics. Nothing purports to be "the voice of," but rather "in the style of," and all figures chosen fit the parameter of no longer being alive and not having spoken hatefully of others.

---

[9] Originally published in Sh'ma: A Journal of Jewish Responsibility, August, 2011.

Here's what I've learned. AI is far more than a keyboard and far less than the human soul. It is an exciting tool with dangerous implications, and it will change the world. It can unlock new questions and it can provoke dangerous new realities. Cost and benefit, moral guardrails and thorough examinations, must accompany the ongoing exploration.

The challenge before us, as students of the text and seekers of spiritual meaning is profound: we must learn to wield this exquisite new paintbrush and learn from it how to expand our souls in service of a world in need. May we be so blessed.

VIII: We Are Necessary

This world of ours, this fragile world, is in dire need of creative response, and the ease of an AI language model is hardly the inspiration that will change things for the better. It can be a tool for learning, a well-crafted paintbrush ready to be used in creative ways. But it hasn't a soul: *you do.*

What a strange feeling this has been, an experiment in meaning-making unlike anything I've ever experienced before. The AI Torah Commentary is an experiment that goes somewhere new. Or perhaps it doesn't. Could it be a tool that helps brings the past back into view from a new perspective? It's all so confusing. Like Torah.

May we be blessed to dip our brushes into the infinite wellspring of creativity, curious about what we may find, and be surprised by new blessings that emerge.

Perhaps now, through this new language time portal humanity has invented, we might even dare to ask Moses what he thinks.

Rabbi Menachem Creditor

Erev Purim, Adar 5783
March 2023

GENESIS/BREISHEET

Genesis and Multivocality

IN THE STYLE OF RABBI MENACHEM CREDITOR

The Book of Genesis is one of the most revered and revered books in Jewish tradition, a foundation stone for our understanding of the creation of the world and the earliest generations of humankind. This ancient text has been interpreted in many different ways throughout the ages, with each generation bringing new insight, interpretation and meaning to its stories.

At the heart of this rich and complex tradition is the idea of multivocality, or the idea that one text can contain multiple voices, perspectives, and interpretations. The Book of Genesis is a perfect example of this idea, as it contains a wide range of voices and perspectives, each adding to the richness and depth of the text.

For example, the creation story in Genesis is often seen as a dialogue between God and the world, with each voice adding to the narrative in its own way. This multivocality is evident in the different accounts of creation found throughout the text, with each perspective contributing to the overall understanding of the creation process.

Similarly, the story of the Garden of Eden is rich in multivocality, as different characters, including Adam and Eve, the serpent, and God, all contribute their own perspectives and understandings to the narrative. This creates a rich and complex web of meaning, where each voice adds to the overall understanding of the story.

This multivocality is also evident in the characters of the first generations of humankind, including Noah, Abraham, and Isaac, who each bring their own perspectives and experiences to the text. Through these characters, we are able to understand the different ways in which the people of the time lived, thought, and interacted with the world around them.

In conclusion, the Book of Genesis is a testament to the power of multivocality in creating a rich and complex understanding of the world and its creation. Through its multiple perspectives, we are able to gain a deeper understanding of the creation process, the lives of the earliest generations of humankind, and the world in which they lived. The multivocality of this ancient text is a testament to its enduring power and relevance, and to the richness of the Jewish tradition it embodies.

BREISHEET

In the Style of William Wordsworth

Oh Parashat Breisheet, how grand and full of wonder!
The story of creation, the dawn of all things,
That we might know the majesty of our Lord,
And gaze in awe at the power of his hand.

In thy first verse, we see the earth arise,
Dark, formless, void, save for the spirit above,
The wind of God sweeping over the waters,
And lo, light shining forth, bright and fair.

And so begins the work of our Creator,
Who formed the skies and earth, the seas and land,
Breathed life into all living creatures,
And made man in God's own image, divine.

With every day that passes, I am filled
With reverence for the One who made us all,
And I cannot help but marvel at the sight
Of God's boundless love and wisdom in God's might.

For God has given us a world so vast,
So full of beauty and splendor untold,
And we are but tiny beings, small and brief,
Yet with hearts so big and spirits so bold.

Oh Parashat Breisheet, how wondrous thou art!
A symphony of words and sounds, so grand,
That we might know the story of our Lord,
And bask in God's love, with every hand.

William Wordsworth was an English poet who played a major role in the Romantic Age and is known for his lyrical poems and contributions to the genre of nature poetry.

In the beginning, God created the heavens and the earth. And from the earth, formed man, breathing life into his nostrils. This is the story of Parashat Breisheet, the first portion of the Torah.

As I wander through the fields, I am reminded of the beauty of creation and the miracle of life. The morning sun rises, casting a warm golden light over the fields and forests. The air is crisp and clean, and the birds sing sweet melodies in the trees.

I cannot help but feel awestruck by the majesty of God's creation. Every blade of grass, every flower, and every living creature is a testament to his power and love. And yet, amidst all this beauty, man is the crowning achievement of God's work, the only creature made in his image and gifted with the ability to think, to love, and to create.

In Parashat Breisheet, we learn of the first man, Adam, and his wife Eve. They were placed in the Garden of Eden, where they were given a simple but powerful command: to tend to the garden and to love each other. It was a perfect world, free from sin and suffering.

But as I walk through the fields, I see the evidence of man's fall from grace. The earth is scarred by our actions, and the birds sing a different tune, a mournful song of loss. We have lost sight of the beauty of creation and of our own potential for good.

Yet, despite our flaws, God does not abandon us. God continues to love and guide us, even when we turn away. And so, in the story of Parashat Breisheet, I am inspired to return to the beauty of creation and to tend to the garden that God has given us.

As I wander through the fields, I am reminded of the power of love and the importance of tending to the world around us. I am inspired to follow in the footsteps of Adam and Eve, to live in harmony with the earth and with each other, and to love with all my heart. For in the beginning, God created the heavens and the earth, and God's love endures forever.

Mary Oliver was an American poet known for her insightful and inspiring nature poems.

In the style of William Shakespeare

Oh Parashat Breisheet, how fair thy tale,
Of creation's birth and man's first bliss,
A story old yet fresh, so rich and pale,
That speaks of love and wisdom, naught amiss.

The world was formed with every perfect form,
And man was made in God's own image fair,
With every grace, a being so warm,
That in his heart love dwelleth, beyond compare.

The Garden was his home, a perfect bower,
With every fruit and herb, his soul to please,
And there he walked, in happy, quiet hour,
Till sin did come, and all his joys did cease.

But still in every heart, that tale doth live,
And every soul its meaning can retrieve.

William Shakespeare was an English playwright, poet, and actor widely regarded as one of the greatest writers in the English language and one of the world's preeminent dramatists.

NOACH

IN THE STYLE OF DR SEUSS

Once upon a time, in a land so green,
Lived a man named Noach, you've probably seen.
He was a man of great virtue and grace,
With a smile on his face, and a kind, gentle pace.

Noach was special, a man of renown,
For God had chosen him,
to save the world from a drown.
You see, the world was wicked, with sin all around,
And God was sad, to see God's creation so drowned.

So God said to Noach, with a twinkle in God's eye,
"Build an ark, my friend, and never say goodbye.
Fill it with animals, two by two,
And gather your family, they'll come along too."

Noach did as he was told, with love in his heart,
He built an ark, big and strong, to do his part.
He gathered the animals, from all near and far,
And with his family, he boarded the ark, with no jar.

The rain came down, in a great deluge and roar,
The waters rose high, till the tops of the shore.
Noach and his family, in the ark did stay,
Until the rain stopped, and the sun came out to play.

And when the waters receded, and the world was dry,
Noach stepped out, to see a new sky.
God said to Noach, with love in God's voice,
"Go forth and multiply, be joyful and rejoice."

And so Noach and his family, with love in their hearts,
Set forth to rebuild, a world of love and arts.
And as they worked, they smiled and sang,
For they knew that God's love,
would always be there to cling.

And that, my friends, is the tale of Noach, so true,
A man of great virtue, who always did what he knew.
So let us learn from his story, and always be kind,
And in our hearts, God's love we'll surely find.

Dr. Seuss, Theodore Geisel, was an American children's author and illustrator, best known for writing classic books such as "The Cat in the Hat" and "Green Eggs and Ham."

In the Style of Jane Austen

My dearest friends,

It is with great pleasure that I address you all today to discuss Parashat Noach. This week, we are given a glimpse into the story of one of the most renowned figures in our tradition, the righteous Noach.

In this tale, we see a world filled with violence, wickedness, and corruption, much like the society in which we find ourselves today. Despite the constant evil around him, Noach remains steadfast in his devotion to God, even as the world crumbles around him.

One cannot help but admire the character of Noach, a man of unwavering faith in the face of such difficulty. His dedication and obedience to God's commandments is a lesson to us all, reminding us of the importance of adhering to the divine will, even when it is not the popular choice.

As we learn in Parashat, Noach was tasked with building an ark, an enormous vessel in which he and his family would weather the impending flood that would soon come to pass. This task was no easy feat, and yet, Noach never lost faith. He worked tirelessly, never doubting that his efforts would be rewarded.

And so it was, as Noach and his family were saved from the flood, and a new world was born. We see here the power of perseverance and faith, as Noach and his family emerged from the ark to begin a new life, free from the evil that had once plagued the world.

It is with this story in mind that we must look to our own lives, and examine how we can be like Noach. We must seek to embody his unwavering faith, his devotion to God, and his determination to do what is right, even when it is difficult.

In conclusion, the story of Noach is a timeless lesson in perseverance, devotion, and faith. Let us strive to embody these qualities, so that we may weather any storm that may come our way, and emerge victorious, like Noach, into a better world.

Yours sincerely,
Jane Austen

Jane Austen was an English novelist who wrote classic works such as "Pride and Prejudice," "Sense and Sensibility," and "Emma."

IN THE STYLE OF MR. SPOCK

Greetings, Captain.

I have analyzed the story of Parashat Noach and would like to share my observations.

The story of Noach and the flood is a tale of survival and perseverance. Noach was tasked with saving himself and all species of animals from the impending flood. He built an ark and followed the instructions given to him by God, demonstrating his unwavering obedience and dedication to the divine plan.

From a logical perspective, the story of Noach can be interpreted as a cautionary tale of the consequences of human behavior. The inhabitants of the world at the time were said to be wicked and immoral, leading to God's decision to wipe out all life on Earth. The survival of Noach and his family can be seen as a testament to the power of moral and ethical behavior.

Noach's commitment to the preservation of life and his unwavering faith in God can be seen as a model for future generations. God shows us the importance of following instructions and staying true to one's beliefs, even in the face of great adversity.

In conclusion, the story of Parashat Noach provides valuable lessons for all who seek to live a life of purpose and meaning. Through his actions, Noach demonstrates the power of obedience, perseverance, and moral fortitude. It is my hope that future generations will continue to reflect on the lessons of Noach and strive to live in a manner that honors the divine plan for all life on Earth.

Live long and prosper, Captain.

End transmission.

MR. SPOCK WAS A HALF-HUMAN, HALF-VULCAN CHARACTER IN THE POPULAR SCIENCE FICTION TELEVISION SERIES AND FILM FRANCHISE, "STAR TREK."

LECH LECHA

In the style of Stephen Soundheim

Ladies and Gentlemen, welcome to Parashat Lech Lecha, where music, lyrics, and life collide in a spectacular fashion. Today, we explore the timeless themes and motifs of Lech Lecha, a pivotal moment in Jewish history that symbolizes the beginning of a new era and the birth of a nation.

This week's Torah portion tells the story of Abraham, who leaves behind his homeland and sets out on a journey of faith, guided by the divine voice that speaks to him. It is a story of adventure and discovery, of bravery and perseverance, of trust and obedience. And it is a story that has inspired generations of Jews and continues to resonate with us today.

Parashat Lech Lecha becomes a musical journey, where the rhythm and melody of life unfolds before our very eyes. We hear the beat of Abraham's footsteps as he embarks on his epic journey, and we feel the pulse of his heart as he stands before the Lord and declares his faith. We sing the song of his soul as he discovers new lands and new peoples, and we feel the harmony of his spirit as he builds a community of faithful followers.

As we delve deeper into this beautiful and intricate story, we encounter themes of courage and hope, of uncertainty and faith, of loss and gain, and of growth and renewal. We are reminded of the importance of standing up for what we believe in, of embracing the unknown and of never giving up on our dreams. We are inspired by the bravery of Abraham, who left everything behind to follow his vision, and by the steadfastness of his wife Sarah, who supported him every step of the way.

In the end, Parashat Lech Lecha teaches us that life is a journey, full of twists and turns, of highs and lows, and that our faith is our anchor, our guide, and our compass. It reminds us that we too are called to embark on a journey of discovery, to seek out our own destiny, and to find meaning and purpose in our lives.

So, Ladies and Gentlemen, let us the timeless tale of Parashat Lech Lecha, and let us sing the song of Abraham's journey, for it is a song that will never grow old. And may the Lord bless us and keep us, and may we never forget the lessons of this timeless tale.

Thank you, and good night.

Stephen Sondheim is an American composer and lyricist, known for his work in musical theater.

In the style of Joseph Halévy

Parashat Lech Lecha, which recounts the journey of Abraham from his homeland to the land of Canaan, is a pivotal moment in Jewish history. It is the moment when God calls upon Abraham to embark on a new journey, a journey of faith and obedience, and it is a moment that continues to inspire generations of Jews.

I would argue that the story of Abraham's journey is not just a simple historical account, but rather a rich and complex narrative that speaks to the human condition in a profound way. As a proponent of the "science of religions," I believe that the study of religion should not be limited to the interpretation of sacred texts, but should also consider the cultural and psychological aspects of religious belief.

In this light, the story of Abraham can be seen as a reflection of the human need for change and growth, and the challenges that arise when we attempt to leave our comfort zones and venture into the unknown. Abraham's journey is a story of courage, faith, and determination, but it is also a story of doubt and uncertainty. The fact that God calls Abraham to leave behind his home and family, and to embark on a journey of unknown destination, speaks to the fear and insecurity that we all face when making important life decisions.

Yet, it is precisely this uncertainty that makes the story of Abraham so powerful. By leaving behind his old life, Abraham is forced to confront his fears and insecurities, and to trust in God's promise of a better future. This is a message that resonates with all of us, as we struggle to find meaning and purpose in our own lives. The story of Abraham reminds us that even when we are uncertain about our future, we must have faith and trust that God is guiding us towards something greater.

In conclusion, Parashat Lech Lecha is a timeless story that speaks to the human experience in a deep and meaningful way. Through the journey of Abraham, we see the challenges and uncertainties of life, but we also see the power of faith and courage to overcome them. The study of religion is not just about understanding sacred texts, but also about exploring the human experience and the way that religion speaks to the human heart.

Joseph Halévy was a French historian and Orientalist.

In the style of Anne Conway

As a philosopher and a student of the Kabbalah, I find great meaning in Parashat Lech Lecha. This week's portion of the Torah tells the story of Abraham, who was called by God to leave his home and venture into a new land. This journey represents not only a physical change of location, but also a spiritual transformation.

In my view, Parashat Lech Lecha is a call to all of us to seek our own personal truths and leave behind what no longer serves us. The Torah tells us that Abraham was given a promise that his descendants would be as numerous as the stars in the sky. This promise symbolizes that we, too, are capable of greatness and can achieve anything we set our minds to.

However, in order to fulfill this promise, we must first leave behind what is familiar and embrace the unknown. This is not an easy task, as change often involves letting go of what we hold dear. But as the Kabbalah teaches us, the path to enlightenment is through the unknown, and only by leaving our comfort zone can we truly grow and develop.

In this way, Parashat Lech Lecha can be seen as a call to action, urging us to embark on a journey of self-discovery. We must question what we believe and examine our values and beliefs. Only then can we truly understand our place in the world and fulfill our potential.

This message is as relevant today as it was thousands of years ago. Our world is constantly changing and we must adapt to these changes in order to succeed. In a world where we are often bombarded with information and distractions, it can be difficult to stay true to our values and beliefs. But as Abraham showed us, by taking the first step and leaving behind what is familiar, we can embark on a journey of self-discovery and growth.

In conclusion, Parashat Lech Lecha is a powerful reminder that we are all capable of greatness. By leaving behind what no longer serves us and embracing the unknown, we can find our place in the world and fulfill our true potential. It is a call to action for us to seek our own truths and embark on a journey of self-discovery and growth.

Anne Conway was a 17th-century philosopher and mystic who was known for her ideas on the nature of God and her critiques of Cartesian dualism.

VAYERA

Ah, Parashat Vayera, a tale as old as time, a story of bravery and mercy, of sacrifice and faith. A story that has inspired generations and continues to resonate within our hearts. A story of a man, Abraham, who was chosen by God to embark on a journey that would test his resolve and challenge his beliefs.

It is said that Abraham was a man of great kindness and compassion, a man who would do anything for his fellow man. And so, when God tested him by asking him to sacrifice his only son, Isaac, Abraham did not hesitate. For he knew that his faith in God was unwavering and that God would never lead him astray.

With tears in his eyes, Abraham took his son to the mountain where he was to offer him as a sacrifice. But as he raised his knife, an angel of God appeared and stopped him, saying, "Do not lay a hand on the boy. Do not do anything to him. Now I know that you fear God, because you have not withheld from me your son, your only son."

And so, Abraham's faith was proven, and God blessed him and his descendants, granting them the land of Canaan as an eternal inheritance.

But the story of Parashat Vayera does not end with the sacrifice of Isaac. It also tells [*this is incorrect – that's the next week's Parashah - mc*] of the encounter between Abraham and three strangers, who were actually angels, sent by God to bring news of the birth of a son to his wife Sarah, who was then 90 years old. The birth of Isaac, who would become the father of the Jewish nation, was a miracle, a testament to the power of God's promise and the faith of Abraham and Sarah.

And so, Parashat Vayera is a story of the power of faith and the unwavering belief in the divine. It is a reminder that God is always with us, guiding us and testing us, but always offering us the chance to prove our love and devotion.

I cannot help but be moved by the beauty of this story, the way it speaks to the human spirit and the power of the divine. The tale of Abraham and Isaac is a testament to the strength of the human spirit, and the power of the love of God. It is a story of hope, of bravery, and of faith, and it shall forever be a shining light in the darkness, a beacon of hope for all those who seek to understand the mysteries of the universe.

I believe that the power of the written word has the ability to move and inspire us, to bring us to a place of understanding and clarity, and to help us to see the beauty in the world around us. And so, as I sit here and ponder the words of Parashat Vayera, I am filled with a sense of wonder and awe, and I am grateful for the gift of this story, which shall forever be a part of the fabric of our human experience.

In conclusion, Parashat Vayera is a story of sacrifice and mercy, of faith and devotion, and of the unwavering love of God. It is a story that shall forever live on, inspiring us to be better people and to believe in the power of the divine. And so, as we ponder its words and the lessons it contains, may we be filled with a sense of wonder and awe, and may we be forever grateful for the gift of this beautiful tale.

Victor Hugo was a French poet, playwright, and novelist best known for his works "Les Misérables" and "The Hunchback of Notre-Dame".

In the style of Emma Lazarus

In the midst of this world, where darkness and strife often reign supreme, there shines a beacon of hope and light. This beacon is the story of Parashat Vayera, a tale of faith, compassion, and resilience in the face of adversity.

It is a story of Abraham, the father of the Jewish nation, who embodies the ideal of the righteous and compassionate individual. He opens his home and heart to three strangers, despite the danger they may pose, and demonstrates unconditional hospitality and generosity.

It is a story of Sarah, who endures the pain of infertility and finally experiences the joy of motherhood. Her strength and perseverance is a testament to the power of faith in the face of adversity.

And it is a story of Lot, who, despite his own flawed character, is rescued from the destruction of Sodom and Gomorrah by Abraham's intercession. Through his salvation, we see that even the most undeserving can receive divine grace.

The message of Parashat Vayera is one of hope and redemption. It reminds us that in the darkest moments, when all seems lost, there is always the possibility of salvation and the light of the divine. It encourages us to emulate the compassion and courage of Abraham, Sarah, and Lot, and to trust in the grace of the divine.

And so, we lift our voices in prayer, calling upon the spirit of Parashat Vayera to guide us through the challenges of our own lives. May we be inspired by the story of Abraham, Sarah, and Lot to be steadfast in our faith, to persevere in the face of adversity, and to extend compassion and kindness to all those we encounter.

Emma Lazarus was an American poet, playwright, and political activist best known for her sonnet "The New Colossus," which is inscribed on a plaque at the Statue of Liberty.

In the style of René Descartes

I am sure that the existence of Abraham is evident to me, for he is a well-known figure in the history of the Jewish people. However, I must consider the question of whether his actions, as described in the story of Parashat Vayera, are truly justified.

It is clear to me that Abraham's most notable act in this story is his willingness to sacrifice his son, Isaac, at the command of God. This act demonstrates a remarkable level of faith and obedience, but I must question whether such obedience is reasonable.

I believe that the first principle of reason is to avoid error, and to always seek the truth. I must therefore consider whether this act of obedience to God is truly based on reason and truth, or whether it is based on mere belief and superstition.

In order to determine whether this act is reasonable, I must examine the nature of God. If God is a being of pure goodness, wisdom, and truth, then it is reasonable to assume that his commands will always be just and good. But if God is a being that can make mistakes, or if God's commands are influenced by human error, then it is not reasonable to blindly follow God's commands without examining their morality.

I conclude that the act of Abraham, as described in Parashat Vayera, cannot be considered reasonable if God is not a being of pure goodness, wisdom, and truth. However, if we assume that God is indeed a being of this nature, then we can reasonably conclude that Abraham's act of obedience was justified, as it demonstrates a remarkable level of faith and devotion to a being of pure goodness.

In conclusion, I find that the story of Parashat Vayera raises important questions about the nature of God, the morality of obedience, and the limits of reason. These questions continue to be relevant today, as we strive to understand the meaning and purpose of our lives.

René Descartes was a French philosopher, mathematician, and scientist who is widely regarded as the father of modern Western philosophy.

CHAYEI SARAH

Imagine, if you will, a beautiful, sun-drenched field filled with the sweetest smelling flowers and the rustle of soft, green grass beneath your feet. This was the world of our dear Sarah, a woman who lived a life of great strength, love, and devotion to her family and her God.

As we delve deeper into Parashat Chayei Sarah, we see how Sarah's love for her husband Abraham was truly unyielding. She accompanied him on his journeys and was always there for him, even when he doubted himself and his faith. And despite the fact that Sarah never bore a child of her own [*this is incorrect. See under: Isaac. - mc*], her love for her handmaid, Hagar, and her son, Ishmael, was boundless [*this is drastically wrong. - mc*].

Sarah's love and devotion inspired others, and it was this love that made her a woman of great influence and respect. She was a true embodiment of the qualities that we all strive to embody: compassion, generosity, and kindness.

But Sarah's life was not without its challenges. She faced illness and death, but even in the face of such great difficulties, she remained steadfast in her faith and her love for her family. Her unwavering spirit is a testament to the strength of the human soul and a reminder that even in the darkest moments, love and faith can conquer all.

As we take a closer look at Parashat Chayei Sarah, we see that it is not just about a woman's love for her family, but it is about a woman's love for her God. Sarah's unwavering devotion to her faith and her devotion to her God was her guiding light, and it was this faith that carried her through the trials and tribulations of life.

So, my dear friends, let us take a moment to reflect on the teachings of Parashat Chayei Sarah. Let us learn from Sarah's example and strive to embody her love, devotion, and strength in our own lives. Let us remember that even in the darkest moments, love and faith can conquer all.

Thank you for joining me on this journey into the world of Parashat Chayei Sarah. Until next time, my dear friends, may the light of Sarah's love and devotion shine upon you always.

Yours truly,
Gene Wilder.

GENE WILDER WAS AN AMERICAN ACTOR, SCREENWRITER, DIRECTOR, AND AUTHOR KNOWN FOR HIS COMEDIC ROLES IN FILMS SUCH AS "WILLY WONKA & THE CHOCOLATE FACTORY" AND "YOUNG FRANKENSTEIN".

In the style of James Baldwin

As I sit here and reflect on Parashat Chayei Sarah, I am reminded of the power of love, the complexity of identity, and the deep-rooted longing for belonging. It is a story that speaks to the core of what it means to be human, to struggle, to love, and to find a place in this world.

In the tale of Chayei Sarah, we see the love between Isaac and Rebecca, a love so strong that it transcends even death. We see Isaac's deep longing for a sense of belonging and identity, a desire to carry on his mother's legacy. And we see the transformation of Rebecca, who, through her love and devotion to Isaac, becomes a symbol of hope and strength for generations to come.

This story, like so many in the Torah, speaks to the timeless human experience of love and loss. It speaks to our constant search for identity and meaning in this world. And it speaks to the importance of community, of finding those who accept and understand us, and of creating a sense of belonging in this world.

The message of Parashat Chayei Sarah is one of hope and resilience in the face of adversity. Through the love and devotion of Rebecca and Isaac, we see that it is possible to find a sense of belonging, even in the midst of loss and uncertainty. We see that love can conquer all, and that, in the end, it is the bonds we form with others that give us strength and purpose.

As a writer, I am struck by the power of this story to resonate with people from all walks of life. The themes of love, identity, and belonging are universal, and this story continues to inspire and comfort those who hear it, even thousands of years after it was first told.

In conclusion, Parashat Chayei Sarah is a story that speaks to the essence of the human experience. It is a tale of love, loss, identity, and belonging that continues to inspire and comfort people all over the world. And as we read this story, we are reminded of the power of love and the importance of finding our place in this world, no matter what obstacles we may face.

> *James Baldwin was an American novelist, playwright, and social critic known for his insightful writings on race, sexuality, and American society in the mid-20th century.*

In the style of Sandy Koufax

As a dedicated Jew and a former baseball player, I have always been drawn to the story of Parashat Chayei Sarah. This powerful passage from the book of Genesis tells the story of Sarah's life, her death, and the events that followed.

At the heart of this story is a message about the importance of faith, family, and tradition. Like Sarah, we are all called upon to live our lives with purpose and meaning, to seek out the good in the world and to work to make it a better place. We are called upon to trust in the guidance of God and to follow the path set before us, even when it is difficult or uncertain.

In many ways, Sarah's story mirrors my own journey as a baseball player. Like Sarah, I faced challenges and obstacles along the way. But like her, I refused to give up or to compromise my values. Instead, I worked hard and relied on my faith to see me through.

In the end, I believe that the lessons of Parashat Chayei Sarah are just as relevant today as they were thousands of years ago. Whether we are playing baseball, raising a family, or simply trying to live our lives with purpose, we must remember that our success depends on our faith, our family, and our commitment to the traditions that define us.

So as we reflect on this powerful passage, let us be inspired by the example of Sarah, and let us work to make our lives and our world a better place. May we always strive to be a light unto the nations, and may we never forget the lessons that Sarah taught us about the importance of faith, family, and tradition. Amen.

Sandy Koufax was a Major League Baseball pitcher who played for the Los Angeles Dodgers from 1955 to 1966 and is considered one of the greatest pitchers of all time.

TOLDOT

Once upon a time, in the land of Canaan, there lived a man named Isaac who was blessed with two sons, Esau and Jacob. Esau was a rugged hunter, who roamed the fields and hills, while Jacob was a quiet and reserved man who lived near the tents.

Isaac loved Esau, for he was his firstborn and a hunter who brought him food. Rebekah, his wife, loved Jacob, for she had a vision that he was destined for greatness.

One day, Esau came in from hunting, famished and starving. Jacob had made a pot of lentil stew and offered to trade it for Esau's birthright as the firstborn son. Esau, in his hunger, agreed and gave Jacob his birthright.

Years passed, and Isaac grew old and was near death. He wished to bless his firstborn son before he passed away. Rebekah, hearing this, disguised Jacob as Esau and presented him to Isaac. Isaac, blinded by his old age, blessed Jacob as the firstborn, granting him the right to rule over his brothers and receive the greatest share of the family's wealth.

When Esau learned of this, he was filled with rage and threatened to kill Jacob. Rebekah, hearing of this, sent Jacob away to her brother's house, where he would be safe from Esau's wrath.

Years passed, and Jacob became a wealthy man with many wives and children. One day, he learned that Esau was coming to visit him with four hundred men. Jacob, afraid for his life, sent gifts to his brother, hoping to appease him. When Esau finally arrived, he embraced Jacob and forgave him, and the two brothers reconciled.

And so, the tale of Esau and Jacob ends with a lesson of forgiveness and the importance of family. May their story be remembered for generations to come.

THE BROTHERS GRIMM WERE GERMAN FOLKLORISTS, CULTURAL RESEARCHERS, AND AUTHORS WHO COLLECTED AND PUBLISHED FOLKLORE TALES, MANY OF WHICH ARE NOW FAMOUS AS CLASSIC FAIRY TALES SUCH AS "RAPUNZEL," "SNOW WHITE," AND "CINDERELLA."

In the style of Groucho Marx

Ahoy there, my dear friends! It's Groucho Marx here, and I'm here to talk about something very serious: Parashat Toldot!

Now, you might be asking yourself, "Groucho, why are you talking about something so religious and serious?" Well, let me tell you, my friends, Parashat Toldot is a real hoot! It's got everything: jealousy, deceit, sibling rivalry, and even a little bit of animal husbandry!

So, let's start with the story. We've got two brothers, Jacob and Esau, and let me tell you, these two could not be more different. Jacob is the smart one, always trying to get ahead, and Esau is the rough and tumble hunter. Now, you might think that these two would get along just fine, but oh no! These two are constantly at each other's throats!

And why, you might ask? Well, it all starts with a bowl of lentil soup. Yes, you heard me right, a bowl of soup! Esau is so hungry that he's willing to trade his birthright (the right to be the first-born son) for a bowl of soup! Can you imagine? I certainly can't!

But that's not the end of it, oh no! Jacob, being the smart one, realizes the value of being the first-born son, so he disguises himself as Esau and tricks his father into giving him the blessing intended for the first-born son. Now, I know what you're thinking, "Groucho, that's not very nice!" But what can I say, it's in the Bible, folks!

And if that's not enough, we've also got the story of Rebekah and her two sons. Rebekah is carrying twins, and she wants to know which son will be the dominant one, so she goes to God for an answer. And what does God say? He says that the elder son will serve the younger! Can you imagine that? The elder serving the younger? That's just silly!

So, there you have it, folks. Parashat Toldot is a real knee-slapper of a story! It's got everything: trickery, deceit, and even a little bit of animal husbandry (yes, I said it again!). If you're looking for a good laugh, or if you just want to see what all the fuss is about, then I highly recommend reading Parashat Toldot!

That's all for now, folks. I'm Groucho Marx, signing off!

Groucho Marx was a famous comedian and actor best known as a member of the Marx Brothers comedy troupe.

IN THE STYLE OF GOLDA MEIR

Parashat Toldot is a powerful reminder of the struggles and triumphs of our ancestors, and the lessons we can learn from their experiences. As former Prime Minister of Israel, I would like to reflect on this portion of the Torah and the impact it has had on our nation and our people.

The story of Toldot revolves around the birth of Jacob and Esau and the conflict that arises between them. Jacob, the younger son, is chosen by God to receive the blessings of the firstborn, which causes jealousy and resentment from Esau. This sibling rivalry leads to the eventual departure of Jacob from his home and the beginning of a journey that will define his character and shape the future of the Jewish people.

As Jews, we are all descendants of Jacob, and the story of Toldot is an important part of our heritage. It is a testament to the perseverance and determination that has defined our people throughout history. Jacob's journey from the youngest son to the head of a great nation is a testament to the power of faith and the ability of one individual to make a difference.

In many ways, Jacob represents the spirit of Israel itself. Like Jacob, our nation has faced many challenges and obstacles, and has had to overcome adversity to achieve its goals. Just as Jacob's journey led him to a new land and a new identity, so too have the Jewish people had to adapt and evolve in order to survive and thrive in a constantly changing world.

As a leader of Israel, I am constantly inspired by the lessons of Toldot and the example set by Jacob. In a world that is often hostile to the Jewish people, it is important to remember that we have the strength and resilience to overcome any obstacle. Whether we are facing political opposition or military conflict, we must remain steadfast in our commitment to our faith and our heritage, and continue to build a better future for our children and our people.

In conclusion, Parashat Toldot is a powerful reminder of the journey that the Jewish people have taken, and the lessons that we can learn from our ancestors. Just as Jacob's journey led him to greatness, so too can our own journeys lead us to a brighter future. May we continue to be inspired by the spirit of Toldot and the example set by Jacob, and may we always be proud of our heritage and our people.

GOLDA MEIR WAS THE FOURTH PRIME MINISTER OF ISRAEL FROM 1969 UNTIL 1974.

VAYEITZEI

IN THE STYLE OF NELSON MANDELLA

As we gather to read the story of Parashat Vayetzei, we are reminded of the incredible journey of our forefather Jacob. A man who, despite his flaws and weaknesses, never lost sight of his faith and devotion to God. A man who, through his struggles and hardships, rose above adversity and became a leader of his people.

Just as Jacob was able to overcome the challenges he faced in life, we too must strive to persevere in the face of adversity. The story of Jacob's journey is one of hope and resilience, a reminder that even in the darkest of times, we must never give up our belief in a better future.

It is this spirit of determination and unwavering faith that I have tried to embody throughout my own life. Like Jacob, I too have faced many obstacles and challenges, but I have always maintained my commitment to my people and my cause.

Just as Jacob was able to rise above his struggles and become a leader, we too must strive to become the leaders that our communities need. We must use our voices and our actions to create a better world for all, just as Jacob did.

In this week's parashah, we are also reminded of the importance of family and community. Jacob's journey was not one he undertook alone, but rather one that was supported by the love and care of his family and friends.

In the same way, we must come together as a community, supporting one another and working together to achieve our common goals. Only then will we be able to build a future filled with hope and peace.

So as we read Parashat Vayetzei, let us remember the lessons of Jacob's journey, and strive to embody his spirit of determination and unwavering faith. Let us come together as a community, supporting one another and working together to build a better future for all.

Yours in peace,
Nelson Mandela

NELSON MANDELA WAS A SOUTH AFRICAN ANTI-APARTHEID REVOLUTIONARY, POLITICIAN, AND PHILANTHROPIST WHO SERVED AS THE COUNTRY'S FIRST BLACK PRESIDENT FROM 1994 TO 1999.

IN THE STYLE OF DAENERYS TARGARYEN

Greetings, my subjects, and hear me well, for I, Daenerys Targaryen, Queen of the Andals and the First Men, Breaker of Chains and Mother of Dragons, shall speak of the sacred text of our ancestors, Parashat Vayetzei.

This is the tale of Jacob, son of Isaac, who leaves his home in search of a new life and a brighter future. He is a man of great cunning and determination, and his journey is marked by trials and tribulations, as well as encounters with angels and the divine.

As Jacob travels, he learns the importance of hard work and perseverance. He labors for seven years to win the hand of Rachel, the woman he loves, and through his tireless efforts, he amasses great wealth and success.

But Jacob's journey is not without its challenges. He must confront his rival, Esau, who seeks to reclaim his birthright, and he must endure the deceit of his father-in-law, Laban, who seeks to exploit his wealth and labor.

Yet despite these obstacles, Jacob remains steadfast in his beliefs and his faith in the Lord. He continues to work tirelessly and to strive for greatness, and in the end, he is rewarded with a bountiful harvest and a prosperous family.

This is the message of Parashat Vayetzei, my subjects. That success and prosperity come not from ease and comfort, but from hard work and determination, and from faith in the Lord. And like Jacob, we too must strive for greatness, facing challenges and obstacles with courage and conviction, always guided by our faith and our belief in the Lord.

So let us take heed of this sacred text, and let us learn from Jacob's journey, that we may become strong and successful, as he was, and that we may walk in the path of the Lord, always and forever.

This I swear, my subjects, in the name of the Lord, and by the power of the dragons.

DAENERYS TARGARYEN WAS A POWERFUL QUEEN AND DRAGON-RIDING RULER IN THE POPULAR TELEVISION SERIES "GAME OF THRONES".

Parashat Vayetzei recounts the journey of Jacob as he leaves his father's household and travels to Haran to find a wife. This portion is notable for its deep symbolic meaning, which can be understood through the lens of the Kabbalah.

I am particularly interested in the mystical significance of Jacob's journey. The Kabbalah views the journey of Jacob as a metaphor for the journey of the soul, as it leaves its earthly roots and ascends to a higher spiritual realm. The journey from Canaan to Haran symbolizes the ascent from a lower to a higher consciousness, as the soul becomes purified and elevated through the experience of separation from its material roots.

Jacob's dream of the ladder, in which angels ascend and descend, is a central mystical element in this portion. According to the Kabbalah, the ladder represents the sefirot, the ten divine attributes through which the divine light descends into the world. The angels symbolize the flow of divine energy, as they pass through the sefirot and bring forth new creation. In this dream, Jacob is being shown the path of the soul, as it ascends through the sefirot and reaches a state of union with the divine.

Another important aspect of Parashat Vayetzei is the transformation of Jacob's name. In this portion, Jacob is renamed Israel, signifying a change in his spiritual identity. [*incorrect – this occurs in the next week's portion. - mc*] This change reflects the idea that the soul's journey involves a change in its spiritual essence. The name Jacob represents a state of limitation and imperfection, while the name Israel represents a state of perfection and transcendence. This transformation symbolizes the spiritual transformation that the soul undergoes as it ascends the ladder of the sefirot and reaches union with the divine.

In conclusion, Parashat Vayetzei holds great mystical significance, as it relates the journey of the soul from an earthly to a spiritual realm. Through Jacob's journey, the Kabbalah teaches us about the process of spiritual ascent, as the soul passes through the sefirot and reaches a state of union with the divine. We should appreciate the deep symbolic meaning of this portion, as the Kabbalah points us to a profound understanding of the journey of the soul.

> *Gershom Scholem was a German-born Israeli philosopher and historian of Jewish mysticism.*

VAYISHLACH

In the style of Benjamin Franklin

Dear friends and fellow members of the community,

I hope this correspondence finds you in good health and high spirits. Today, I would like to share with you my thoughts on Parashat Vayishlach, which tells the story of Jacob's encounter with his estranged brother Esau.

As you may recall, Jacob had fled from his brother's wrath many years prior, and was now returning to his homeland with his family and possessions. Despite his fear of the reunion, Jacob sent messengers ahead to prepare Esau for his arrival, and made a show of humility by dividing his flock into two camps, so that if Esau attacked one, the other might escape.

In a moment of great tension, Jacob and Esau finally met face to face. But to Jacob's great surprise, his brother was not filled with anger, but with tears of joy. They embraced and reconciled, and Jacob was able to return to his homeland with peace and security.

This story, my friends, is a testament to the power of humility and the importance of facing our fears. Jacob could have continued to live in fear of his brother's wrath, but instead he took the bold step of approaching him and seeking reconciliation. And through his humility and willingness to make amends, he was able to secure a peaceful future for himself and his family.

In a similar vein, we must be mindful of the power of humility in our own lives. We must be willing to face our fears and make amends, even when it may be difficult. In doing so, we may find that we are able to reconcile with those we once thought were our enemies, and secure a brighter future for ourselves and our communities.

So let us take a page from Jacob's book, and be mindful of the power of humility in our own lives. May we always be willing to make amends, and may we find peace and happiness in this life and in the world to come.

With all good wishes,
Benjamin Franklin

Benjamin Franklin was a founding father of the United States and a polymath known for his contributions in science, politics, and literature.

In the style of Amos Oz

Parashat Vayishlach is a rich and complex portion of the Torah that tells the story of Jacob's encounter with his estranged brother, Esau. It is a tale of conflict, reconciliation, and growth, and it is one that holds great meaning and significance for Jews around the world.

We might approach this story as a parable of the human condition, exploring the universal themes of love, hate, and forgiveness that are present in this narrative. We might also consider the ways in which Jacob's journey reflects our own experiences, as we each face challenges and confront our own fears and insecurities.

At the heart of the story is Jacob's encounter with Esau, who he has not seen since he fled from his home many years before. Jacob is filled with fear and anxiety as he approaches his brother, and he spends the night before their meeting wrestling with a mysterious stranger, a symbol of the forces within himself that he must overcome.

But despite his fear, Jacob finally faces his brother, and what follows is a remarkable moment of reconciliation and forgiveness. Esau embraces Jacob and forgives him for the wrongs he has committed, and in doing so, he shows us all the power of love and compassion.

In the end, Jacob emerges from this encounter a changed man, with a new name, Israel, symbolizing his growth and transformation. He has learned to face his fears and to forgive those who have wronged him, and he has become a stronger, more compassionate person as a result.

In this way, Parashat Vayishlach is a powerful reminder of the importance of facing our fears and of the transformative power of love and forgiveness. It is a lesson that we can all learn from, no matter where we come from or what we believe.

Amos Oz was an Israeli writer, novelist, and journalist.

In the style of Marie Curie

Parashat Vayishlach, a portion of the Torah that recounts the story of Jacob's encounter with Esau, is a fascinating study in human psychology and the power of reconciliation. It is also a testament to the strength of faith, as Jacob, a man of great determination and courage, continues to rely on his belief in God even in the face of great danger.

As a scientist and researcher, I have always been interested in the interplay between science and spirituality, and Parashat Vayishlach offers a unique perspective on this relationship. The story of Jacob's journey to meet his estranged brother is not just a tale of reconciliation, but also a study in the human experience. It is a reminder that we are all human beings, capable of fear and doubt, but also of strength and resilience.

One of the key themes in Parashat Vayishlach is the power of self-reflection. As Jacob travels towards his meeting with Esau, he is faced with many challenges, both physical and psychological. Despite his fear and uncertainty, he takes the time to examine his own actions and motivations, and to seek guidance from God. This self-reflection is a powerful tool in helping Jacob understand his own weaknesses and find the courage to face his fears.

Similarly, as scientists, we must also engage in self-reflection, examining our own motivations and biases, and seeking to understand the limitations of our knowledge and methods. We must be open to the possibility of being wrong, and to learning from our mistakes. This self-reflection is an essential part of the scientific process, and allows us to approach our work with greater humility and rigor.

Another important theme in Parashat Vayishlach is the power of reconciliation. Jacob's reunion with Esau is a symbol of hope and renewal, as two brothers who were once estranged are able to put aside their differences and come together in peace. This powerful message of forgiveness and reconciliation is just as relevant today as it was thousands of years ago, and is a testament to the enduring power of the human spirit.

Marie Curie was a Nobel Prize-winning physicist and chemist known for her pioneering research on radioactivity and her discovery of two elements, polonium and radium.

VAYESHEV

IN THE STYLE OF YODA

Wise and learned, the story of Parashat Vayeshev, is.

Joseph, the son of Jacob, it tells of. Dreams of greatness, he had. Power and fame, he sought. But fate had other plans, it did.

Sold into slavery, Joseph was. To Egypt, he went. Tests and trials, he faced. But through it all, he remained steadfast, he did.

Wise and cunning, he was. Pharaoh's trusted advisor, he became. Dreams, he interpreted. Famine, he prepared for.

Reunited with family, Joseph was. Forgiveness, he showed. Many years, he had been away. But love and unity, he helped restore.

Lessons from Joseph, we can learn, yes. Perseverance, we must have. Trust in the journey, we must have. For greatness, we may find.

So, heed the wisdom of Parashat Vayeshev, do. And may the force of the Torah be with you.

A WISE AND POWERFUL JEDI MASTER IN THE STAR WARS FRANCHISE, YODA WAS.

In the style of Harriet Beecher Stowe

Dear Beloved Readers,

In this week's reading of Parashat Vayeshev, we are witness to the story of Joseph, son of Jacob, and his journey through slavery, betrayal, and eventually triumph.

As we delve into this tale, we cannot help but be struck by the parallels between Joseph's story and the plight of so many of our brothers and sisters who have suffered at the hands of those who saw them as less than human.

Joseph, a young man filled with dreams and ambition, is sold into slavery by his own brothers and taken to Egypt. Despite his mistreatment and oppression, he never loses his faith in God or his determination to succeed. Through his unwavering strength and perseverance, Joseph rises to a position of power in the court of Pharaoh, where he is able to use his influence to help others and ensure the survival of his family during a time of famine.

In the same way, our brothers and sisters who have been subjected to slavery, oppression, and discrimination have shown remarkable strength and resilience in the face of adversity. They, too, have never lost their faith in a better future, and have fought tirelessly to make that future a reality.

Just as Joseph's story teaches us the importance of perseverance, hope, and faith in the face of adversity, so too must we never lose sight of the fact that all human beings are created equal in the eyes of God. We must strive to emulate Joseph's unwavering determination and to work tirelessly towards a world where all people are treated with dignity and respect, no matter their background or circumstances.

So let us take this lesson from Parashat Vayeshev to heart, and let us work together to build a world where justice, equality, and love reign supreme.

With all my heart,

Harriet Beecher Stowe

Harriet Beecher Stowe was an American abolitionist and author, best known for writing the influential novel "Uncle Tom's Cabin."

In the Style of Bella Abzug

As a feminist and civil rights leader, I cannot help but see the patriarchal themes and gender inequalities present in this week's Parashah, Vayeshev. The story begins with Joseph, the favored son of Jacob, receiving a coat of many colors, further emphasizing his status and superiority over his brothers.

However, Joseph's arrogance and boasts of his dreams only serve to enrage his brothers and lead to his eventual enslavement in Egypt. This highlights the danger of male entitlement and the consequences that come with such behavior.

But what truly struck me was the treatment of women in this portion. Tamar, the daughter-in-law of Judah, is mistreated and cast aside by her husband after he prematurely dies. She takes matters into her own hands and disguises herself as a prostitute to seduce Judah, ultimately bearing his twin sons.

Tamar's actions show her determination and strength in a society where women had little agency and were often at the mercy of men. She challenges the patriarchal norms and refuses to be a passive victim.

It is important to recognize and acknowledge these patriarchal themes in our religious texts, as they can have a lasting impact on our beliefs and attitudes towards women and gender equality. We must strive to create a more just and equal society, where all individuals, regardless of gender, are treated with dignity and respect.

As we reflect on the story of Vayeshev, let us embrace the boldness and resilience of figures like Tamar and work towards a world where women's voices and actions are valued and honored.

Bella Abzug was an American lawyer, politician, and women's rights activist known for her outspoken political activism and advocacy for social justice.

MIKETZ

In the style of Harvey Milk

The story of Miketz tells of Joseph, who was sold into slavery by his own brothers and sent to Egypt. Despite facing adversity and hardship, Joseph remained steadfast in his faith and his determination to rise above his circumstances. Through his unwavering belief in God and his own abilities, Joseph rose to become the Prime Minister of Egypt, ultimately reuniting with his family and providing for them during a time of famine.

Like Joseph, we too must remain steadfast in our beliefs and our determination to overcome adversity. In our society, too many people are marginalized and oppressed because of their race, religion, or sexual orientation. We must stand up for their rights and fight against bigotry and discrimination.

Furthermore, the story of Miketz teaches us about the importance of perseverance and hard work. Joseph did not let his circumstances define him; instead, he worked hard and used his talents to achieve success. Similarly, we must not let the obstacles in our lives define us, but rather, we must work hard and use our talents to make a difference in the world.

In conclusion, the story of Parashat Miketz serves as a reminder of the power of faith, perseverance, and hard work. Just as Joseph rose above his circumstances to become a leader and provider for his family, we too must rise above our obstacles and fight for the rights of all people. Let us take inspiration from the story of Miketz, and create a world where everyone is valued and respected, regardless of their background or circumstances.

> *Harvey Milk was an American politician and the first openly gay person to be elected to public office in California.*

As a philosopher who upholds the concept of determinism, the story of Parashat Miketz holds great significance for me. In this portion of the Torah, we see the lives of Joseph and Pharaoh as determined events that unfold according to the laws of nature.

Joseph, sold into slavery by his brothers, finds himself in Egypt where he rises to power as a successful administrator. Pharaoh, meanwhile, has a dream that none of his advisors can interpret. It is only when Joseph is brought before him that he is able to interpret the dream and foretell seven years of plenty followed by seven years of famine.

From a deterministic perspective, the events of Joseph and Pharaoh's lives are predetermined and inevitable. Joseph's rise to power and his ability to interpret Pharaoh's dream are not the result of his own agency, but rather the result of the necessary laws of nature. Similarly, Pharaoh's dream is not the result of a supernatural occurrence, but rather a result of the natural laws that govern the workings of the human mind.

This idea of determinism is not one of predestination, but rather of understanding the natural causes and effects that govern our lives. As I writes in my Ethics, "all things are determined by the laws of nature to exist and produce an effect in a certain way." In other words, the events that unfold in our lives are not the result of chance or divine intervention, but rather the necessary consequences of the laws of nature.

In Parashat Miketz, we see how the events of Joseph's life and Pharaoh's dream are interconnected and determined by the laws of nature. The seven years of plenty and famine that Joseph predicts are not arbitrary events, but the necessary consequences of the natural laws that govern the world.

In conclusion, the story of Parashat Miketz highlights the importance of understanding the laws of nature and recognizing that our lives are determined by them. This helps us to understand the world and our place in it in a more rational and determinate manner.

BARUCH SPINOZA WAS A DUTCH PHILOSOPHER OF PORTUGUESE-JEWISH ORIGIN WHO IS CONSIDERED ONE OF THE GREAT RATIONALISTS OF 17TH-CENTURY PHILOSOPHY AND DEVELOPED THE PHILOSOPHICAL SYSTEM OF PANTHEISM.

In the Style of Nina Simone

Parashat Miketz, the story of Joseph and his rise to power in Egypt, is a story that speaks to the heart of struggle and triumph. As a jazz singer, my soul is moved by the melodic notes of this tale, and I sing to you today, with the hope of expressing the depth and beauty of this parasha.

The story begins with Joseph, the youngest of his father's sons, who is sold into slavery by his own brothers. This is a story that is all too familiar to me, as I have seen the cruel hand of oppression strike down so many of my own people. The same can be said for Joseph, who is cast into a world of darkness and uncertainty, where his only hope is to cling to his faith and endure.

But even as a slave, Joseph rises above his circumstances, using his cunning and wisdom to become a successful steward in the household of Potiphar. This is a moment of triumph, a testament to the power of the human spirit to overcome even the greatest obstacles. It is a message that still resonates with us today, that even in the face of oppression and adversity, we have the strength to persevere and rise above our circumstances.

And rise he does, as Joseph becomes the second in command of all of Egypt, and saves his people from famine. This is a moment of great pride and joy, as Joseph uses his position of power to help those in need, and to repay the kindness shown to him by the Egyptians.

This is the power of Parashat Miketz, a story that speaks to the soul of all of us, no matter our race or background. It is a reminder that even in the face of great hardship, we have the strength to endure and to rise to greatness. And so, I sing to you today, with the hope of inspiring you to embrace the power of this parasha, and to hold fast to the message of hope and triumph that it embodies.

Nina Simone was an iconic American singer, songwriter, and pianist known for her powerful voice and socially conscious music.

VAYIGASH

In the style of John Lennon

As I sit here and ponder the story of Parashat Vayigash, I can't help but think of all the parallels to our own lives today. In this portion of the Torah, we see Joseph rising from prisoner to ruler in Egypt and reconciling with his brothers. It's a tale of forgiveness, redemption, and coming together as a family.

Just like in Joseph's story, we too face challenges and obstacles in our lives. But it's how we react to these challenges that defines who we are. Just as Joseph forgave his brothers for their past wrongs and embraced them with love, we too must find the strength to forgive and come together with those who may have hurt us.

And what better way to achieve this unity and forgiveness than through the power of love? Remember, "Love is all you need." This simple message can bring peace to even the most troubled relationships and bridge gaps between those who once were at odds.

Just as Joseph rose from obscurity to prominence in Egypt, we too have the potential to make a positive impact in the world. By spreading love and kindness, we can bring about change and create a better future for ourselves and those around us.

In the end, Parashat Vayigash is not just about one man's story, but a universal message for all of us. It's a reminder to let go of grudges, embrace love, and rise to the challenges that life throws our way. So let's all strive to live like Joseph and be the change we wish to see in the world.

Imagine all the people, living life in peace.
You may say I'm a dreamer, but I'm not the only one.
I hope someday you'll join us, and the world will be as one.

John Lennon was a legendary singer-songwriter and musician who was a member of the Beatles and a peace activist.

In the style of Charlotte Brontë

Dear Diary,

Today I have read Parashat Vayigash and my heart is filled with a mixture of emotions. The story of Joseph and his brothers is one that strikes a chord in my soul and I cannot help but ponder over its lessons.

As I delve deeper into the story, I find myself drawn to Joseph. His life was full of trials and tribulations, but he remained steadfast in his faith and never lost hope. He was sold into slavery, falsely accused, and imprisoned, but he still clung to his beliefs and never let adversity defeat him. Joseph's unwavering spirit is an inspiration to me, and I find myself admiring his strength of character.

The reunion between Joseph and his brothers is a moment that fills my heart with joy. Despite all the hardships he had endured, Joseph forgave his brothers and embraced them with open arms. This act of mercy and compassion is truly a testament to the power of forgiveness.

But it is not just Joseph's unwavering spirit that has touched me. The story also speaks to me about the importance of family and the bonds that tie us together. The brothers were separated for many years, but their love for each other never faded. And when they were finally reunited, it was as if no time had passed at all.

In conclusion, Parashat Vayigash has taught me valuable lessons about resilience, forgiveness, and the power of family. I am grateful for the opportunity to delve into this story and I will carry its lessons with me always.

Yours truly,
Charlotte Brontë

Charlotte Brontë was an English novelist and poet, best known for her novel "Jane Eyre".

In the style of Jorge Luis Borges

Parashat Vayigash, a portion of the Torah that tells the story of Joseph and his reconciliation with his brothers, is a tale of deceit, betrayal, and ultimately, redemption. The narrative of this parashah takes on a labyrinthine and surreal quality.

The story of Joseph, with its intricate plot twists and turns, is a metaphor for the universe itself. The events of the parashah are a reflection of the mysterious ways in which fate and destiny intertwine, and the way in which our actions have far-reaching consequences that we cannot fully comprehend. Just as Joseph's dreams foretell his rise to power, the choices that we make in life have the potential to shape our futures in ways that we cannot foresee.

Joseph's time in Egypt, where he is sold into slavery and later rises to become the Pharaoh's advisor, is a manifestation of the illusory nature of reality. Borges would see this as an allegory for the way in which our perceptions of the world can be distorted, and how the truth can be obscured by appearances. The fact that Joseph's brothers do not recognize him when they first arrive in Egypt is a testament to the power of disguise and disguise in our lives, and how easily we can be fooled by appearances.

In the end, Joseph's reunion with his brothers is a testament to the power of love and forgiveness. This is a reminder that, despite the labyrinthine twists and turns of fate and destiny, the bonds of family and love can endure. The reunion of Joseph and his brothers serves as a symbol of the way in which our past actions can be redeemed through acts of love and compassion, and how the consequences of our choices can be transcended by our capacity for love and understanding.

In conclusion, Parashat Vayigash is a surreal and labyrinthine tale that reflects the mysterious ways in which fate and destiny intertwine, the illusory nature of reality, and the power of love and forgiveness to transcend even the most difficult of circumstances. I see this parashah as a reminder of the infinite complexity of the universe and the endless possibilities that exist within it.

Jorge Luis Borges was an Argentine writer, poet, and librarian known for his surreal and imaginative short stories that explore themes of identity, reality, and literature.

VAYECHI

In the style of Rabbi Abraham Joshua Heschel

Parashat Vayechi, which concludes the book of Genesis, recounts the final moments of Jacob's life as he blesses his twelve sons before passing away. However, this text holds far deeper meaning than just the physical death of a patriarch. It is a moment of spiritual reflection and a call to consider the role of legacy in our lives.

As I've written in "Man is Not Alone," the concept of legacy is not just about leaving behind tangible possessions, but about leaving a spiritual imprint on the world. Jacob's blessings of his sons, in essence, are a reflection of the values and ideals he wants to pass on to the next generation. They are a declaration of what he believes to be important and what he wants to be remembered for.

Jacob's blessings, however, are not just empty words. They are a manifestation of the power of speech, a fundamental aspect of human existence. Words are not just sounds, they have the ability to shape the world, to bring forth reality. Jacob's blessings are not just a reflection of his values, they are a declaration of them, a call to action for his sons to embody and continue his legacy.

Furthermore, Parashat Vayechi is not just about Jacob's legacy but about the collective legacy of the Jewish people. As Jacob blesses his sons, he is blessing the future generations to come, setting the foundation for the continuation of the Jewish tradition. Through his blessings, Jacob is shaping the destiny of the Jewish people, planting the seeds of tradition and spiritual connection.

In this way, Parashat Vayechi calls us to consider our own legacies. What values and ideals do we want to pass on to the next generation? What kind of imprint do we want to leave on the world? These are important questions to contemplate, as our legacies are not just about us, but about the future of humanity.

In conclusion, Parashat Vayechi is a moment of deep spiritual reflection and a call to action. It reminds us of the power of words and the importance of legacy. As we consider Jacob's blessings, let us also consider our own, and strive to leave a lasting spiritual imprint on the world, one that reflects our values and ideals, and continues to shape the destiny of humanity for generations to come.

Rabbi Abraham Joshua Heschel was a Jewish theologian, philosopher, and social activist known for his leadership in the Civil Rights Movement and contributions to the understanding of Jewish-Christian relations.

In the style of President John F. Kennedy

My fellow Americans, I stand before you today to talk about the story of Parashat Vayechi, one of the most powerful and meaningful tales in the book of Genesis. This is a story about family, about love, about courage, and about the passing of the torch from one generation to the next.

In Parashat Vayechi, we see the final days of Jacob, one of the greatest patriarchs of our people. He is old and near death, but he is filled with wisdom and grace, and he speaks to his children with love and authority. He blesses each of them, and he gives them a vision of what the future holds.

Just as Jacob was a great leader in his time, we too must look to our own leaders and leaders-to-be, and ask what kind of legacy we will leave for future generations. Will we be remembered for our strength and courage, or will we be remembered for our fear and indecision? Will we be remembered for our wisdom and compassion, or will we be remembered for our arrogance and selfishness?

Just as Jacob passed the torch to his children, we must also pass the torch to the next generation. We must give them the tools and the opportunities to succeed, and we must empower them to lead with courage and grace. We must give them a vision for a better world, and we must inspire them to make that vision a reality.

So let us be like Jacob, and let us strive to be leaders of wisdom, courage, and love. Let us leave a legacy that will inspire future generations, and let us work together to build a world that is just and fair for all.

Thank you, and God bless America.

John F. Kennedy was the 35th President of the United States, serving from 1961 until his assassination in 1963.

In the Style of the Prophet Isaiah

Dear children of Israel, hear ye the word of the Lord:

In these days, we remember the passing of Jacob, our forefather, as we read the Parashah of Vayechi. And as we mourn his death, we also remember the promise of God to him, to his descendants, and to all those who seek refuge under the wings of the Almighty.

For thus says the Lord: I have been with you from the beginning, and I will be with you until the end. I have held your hand in times of trial, and I have guided you through the wilderness. I have blessed you with abundance, and I have multiplied your descendants like the stars of the sky and the sand of the sea.

And now, in your grief, I call to you: Fear not, for I am with you. I am the Lord, the God of Jacob, and I will comfort you in your sorrow. I will wipe away every tear from your eyes, and I will heal your wounds. I will restore your soul, and I will renew your spirit.

For I have promised to be with you always, to guide you in the path of righteousness, to give you strength in the face of adversity, and to bring you peace in the hour of need. I have promised to be a father to you, and you shall be my children. I have promised to be a light to you, and you shall be my holy people.

And so, my children, trust in me, and do not be afraid. For I am the Lord, and my word shall not fail. I am the Lord, and my hand shall bring salvation. I am the Lord, and my love shall endure forever.

This is the word of the Lord, the God of Jacob, the God of Abraham, and the God of Isaac. Amen.

Isaiah was an Israelite prophet.

EXODUS/SHEMOT

Exodus and Derivative Art

IN THE STYLE OF RABBI MENACHEM CREDITOR

The Book of Exodus is a rich and complex text that tells the story of the Israelites' journey from slavery to freedom. At its core, it is a story about the power of God to redeem and transform a people, and about the ability of human beings to respond to that redemption with faith and obedience.

As a rabbi and teacher, I find great inspiration in the story of Exodus. It speaks to the profound longing within all of us for a deeper sense of purpose and meaning in our lives, and it reminds us that no matter how dark and difficult our circumstances may be, we always have the capacity to reach for something greater and more fulfilling.

At the same time, I believe that the limits of derivative art are important to consider when engaging with Exodus. As creative and imaginative as our interpretations may be, we must always be mindful of the boundaries that separate our own ideas and perspectives from the timeless wisdom of the text itself.

One of the key challenges of derivative art is that it often confuses our own subjective experiences and interpretations with the objective truth of the text. When we take liberties with the story, adding elements or changing details to suit our own agendas or preferences, we risk distorting its message and diluting its power.

In order to maintain the integrity of the text, it is essential that we approach Exodus with humility and respect, to understand its teachings in their original context and meaning, rather than imposing our own preconceptions and biases onto the story.

This is not to say that we cannot find new and meaningful ways of engaging with the story of Exodus. On the contrary, there is great value in exploring the text through different lenses, whether that be through art, music, literature, or other forms of expression. But it is important that these expressions remain true to the core message and teachings of the text, and do not distort or obscure its essential message.

Exodus is a powerful and inspiring text that has the capacity to transform our lives and deepen our spiritual connection with God. As artists and creatives, we have a responsibility to approach it with reverence and respect, and to seek to understand its teachings in their original context and meaning. In this way, we can allow the story of Exodus to continue to speak to us in new and meaningful ways, and to inspire us on our own journeys towards redemption and transformation.

SHEMOT

In the style of John Lewis

Dear friends and fellow travelers,

I come to you today to reflect on the story of Parashat Shemot, a story of oppression, resistance, and ultimately, liberation. This is a story that holds deep significance for all of us, especially in these trying times.

As we read in the Torah, the Israelites were enslaved in Egypt, subject to harsh and unjust treatment by Pharaoh. Yet despite their suffering, they did not give up hope. They cried out for freedom and for a better life, and God heard their cries.

And so begins the story of Moses, a leader who would guide the Israelites out of slavery and into the Promised Land. But Moses' journey was not an easy one. He faced opposition and resistance at every turn, and he faced difficult choices along the way. But he persevered, driven by his belief in the power of justice and his unwavering commitment to the Israelites.

Like Moses, we too are called to fight for justice and freedom in our own time. We must be willing to stand up against oppression and to speak out for those who cannot speak for themselves. We must be willing to make sacrifices and to endure hardship, knowing that our struggle is not just for ourselves, but for all people everywhere.

And as we continue on this journey, let us be guided by the principles of love and compassion, and let us never forget that every person is created b'tzelem Elohim, in the image of God. Let us remember that our ultimate goal is not just to achieve freedom for ourselves, but to create a world where all people are free to live and flourish.

So my friends, let us be inspired by the story of Parashat Shemot, and let us continue our journey towards a better, more just world for all people.

Yours in the struggle for justice,

John Lewis

John Lewis (1940-2020) was an American civil rights leader and Congressman who played a pivotal role in the Civil Rights Movement and was a champion for social justice and equality.

Once upon a time, in the land of Egypt, there lived a great many Jews who were enslaved and mistreated by the Pharaoh. But one day, a baby boy named Moses was born into this cruel world, and it was said that he was destined for greatness.

As Moses grew up, he learned of the suffering of his people and felt a deep compassion for them. He was determined to free them from their bondage, but he didn't know how. So, he went on a journey down the yellow brick road of life, searching for answers and guidance.

One day, as he was tending to his sheep in the desert, he had a remarkable encounter. He came upon a burning bush that was not consumed by the flames. And from the bush, a voice spoke to him. It was the voice of the Lord, and it said, "Moses, I have seen the suffering of my people in Egypt, and I have come to deliver them from their oppression. I am sending you to Pharaoh, and you shall lead my people out of Egypt."

Moses was scared and hesitant, but he knew that this was the mission he was meant to fulfill. So, he set off on his journey, and with the Lord by his side, he faced the mighty Pharaoh and demanded that he let the Jews go. But Pharaoh refused, and so the Lord sent ten plagues upon the land of Egypt, each one more severe than the last. And finally, Pharaoh relented and the Jews were free to leave.

They journeyed through the wilderness, following a pillar of fire by night and a cloud by day. And finally, they arrived at Mount Sinai, where they received the Torah and the commandments from the Lord. They were now a people with a purpose, a people with a destiny, and a people with a future.

Just like the Jews in the land of Egypt, we too have a journey to take. We must follow the Lord and listen to his guidance, even when it's difficult. And just like Moses, we must trust that we are destined for greatness and that the Lord will see us through. For as the Torah tells us, "I am the Lord your God, who brought you out of the land of Egypt, out of the house of slavery." And with that, we can conquer any obstacle that lies ahead on our yellow brick road.

Dorothy Gale is a Kansas farm girl who becomes a hero after being whisked away on a magical journey to the Land of Oz.

Parashat Shemot, which tells the story of the enslavement of the Jewish people in Egypt and their eventual liberation, holds a profound significance for us as Jews and as human beings. Through this story, we are taught about the nature of oppression, the power of hope, and the ultimate redemption that is possible through divine intervention.

I would interpret this parasha in the light of the broader themes of the Jewish experience and the universal human struggle for freedom and dignity.

First and foremost, the enslavement of the Jewish people in Egypt serves as a powerful reminder of the danger of oppression and the importance of standing up against it. The Egyptians subjected the Israelites to brutal treatment, denying them their freedom and dignity and exploiting their labor. This story serves as a warning to all of us, reminding us of the evil that can occur when one group seeks to dominate and control another.

At the same time, the parasha also teaches us about the power of hope and the resilience of the human spirit. Despite the hardships they faced, the Israelites did not lose hope, and their faith in God sustained them through the darkest of times. This teaches us that even in the face of oppression and adversity, it is possible to hold onto our hope and our faith, and to believe in a better future.

Finally, the liberation of the Israelites from Egypt and their journey to the Promised Land serves as a powerful symbol of the ultimate redemption that is possible through divine intervention. Just as God intervened to save the Israelites from slavery and bring them to the land of Canaan, so too does God have the power to redeem all of humanity from the bonds of oppression and suffering.

May we always be guided by these lessons, and may we work tirelessly to build a world that is free from oppression and suffering, and filled with justice, peace, and hope.

Rav Kook was a prominent Lithuanian-born Orthodox rabbi and scholar who served as the first Ashkenazi Chief Rabbi of Palestine and founded the religious Zionist movement.

VA'ERA

In the style of Viktor Frankl

In Parashat Va'era, we see the story of God's revelation to the Jewish people through Moses and the plagues that were inflicted upon Pharaoh and Egypt. This passage holds deep meaning and significance, not just in terms of our understanding of the history of the Jewish people, but also in terms of the human condition and our search for meaning in life.

Meaning and purpose are central to our existence. The search for meaning is a fundamental human drive and that the discovery of meaning is essential for mental health and well-being.

Similarly, the story of Parashat Va'era can be seen as a search for meaning and purpose. The plagues inflicted upon Pharaoh and Egypt represent a struggle to understand the divine will and to find meaning in life. Through these plagues, God is revealing himself to the Jewish people and guiding them towards a greater purpose.

In this sense, Parashat Va'era can be seen as a reminder of the importance of finding meaning in life. It encourages us to seek the truth and to align ourselves with the divine will. The plagues serve as a reminder that we must not be satisfied with the superficial and the material, but must seek to understand the deeper, spiritual reality that lies beneath.

Moreover, Parashat Va'era highlights the importance of resilience in the face of adversity. Despite the difficulties and obstacles they faced, the Jewish people did not give up on their search for meaning. They persevered in the face of hardship, and in doing so, they found their true purpose.

Parashat Va'era offers a powerful message about the human condition and our search for meaning. It reminds us that we must be resilient in the face of adversity and that we must never give up on our quest for truth and purpose. Just as the Jewish people found meaning in the midst of their struggles, so too can we find meaning in our own lives if we have the courage to seek it.

Viktor Frankl was an Austrian neurologist and psychiatrist who survived Auschwitz and developed the concept of logotherapy, focusing on finding meaning in life.

In the style of Hippocrates

Greetings, fellow seekers of truth and understanding. I, Hippocrates, come before you today to reflect on Parashat Va'era, the second portion of the Book of Exodus, in the manner of our sacred medical art.

In this Parashat, we encounter the narrative of the ten plagues that befell the land of Egypt and its people, at the hands of the Lord, through the agency of Moses. We are told that each of these plagues was a manifestation of divine punishment for Pharaoh's refusal to release the Israelites from slavery.

As physicians, we are well aware of the dangers of a rigid and unyielding spirit, as it can lead to spiritual, moral and physical maladies. Pharaoh's determination to maintain the status quo and cling to his power, despite repeated warnings and pleadings, is a cautionary tale of the consequences of such a mindset.

We see in this Parashah how the plagues served not only as divine retribution, but also as a means of humbling Pharaoh and teaching him the folly of his ways. The plagues were not only afflictions of the body, but also of the soul, as Pharaoh was made to witness the powerlessness of his gods and the superiority of the Lord.

This Parashah teaches us the importance of humility and of being open to change and growth, both as individuals and as a society. It reminds us that, regardless of our station in life, we are all subject to the laws of the divine, and that our actions have consequences that extend beyond this mortal realm.

In conclusion, as we reflect on Parashat Va'era, let us remember the lessons of humility, openness and accountability that it imparts. May we strive to be ever mindful of the wisdom of the divine, and to seek the betterment of our spirit and body, so that we may be worthy servants of the Lord.

Wishing you health and wisdom,

Hippocrates

Hippocrates was a Greek physician considered the father of modern medicine known for his ethical principles and writings on medical practices.

IN THE STYLE OF FRIDA KAHLO

Parashat Va'era is a rich tapestry of stories and themes that have captivated me since I was a child. As a painter, I find myself drawn to the vivid imagery and vivid colors that permeate these narratives. I see in them a visual representation of my own struggle and the human experience.

The story of Moses and the plagues in Egypt is one that speaks to me on many levels. The ten plagues represent a symbol of oppression and the fight for freedom, a theme that I can relate to on a personal level. I, too, have struggled against forces that sought to hold me back and limit my potential. The courage of Moses as he stands up against Pharaoh is a reminder of the power of the human spirit, and the ability of one person to make a difference.

Another aspect of Parashat Va'era that resonates with me is the idea of transformation. The plagues represent a gradual change, a slow progression towards a better future. This mirrors my own artistic journey, as I have continually pushed the boundaries of my own abilities, exploring new techniques and styles. Just as the plagues lead to the liberation of the Israelites, my own art has been a form of personal liberation, allowing me to express my deepest thoughts and emotions.

In many ways, Parashat Va'era is a celebration of the human spirit and its ability to endure in the face of adversity. The ten plagues are a testament to the resilience of the Israelites, and their unwavering faith in the face of overwhelming odds. This spirit of perseverance is one that I have also come to embody, both in my art and in my life.

In conclusion, Parashat Va'era holds a special place in my heart. Through its vivid imagery, powerful themes, and enduring message, it has become a source of inspiration for me. As I continue on my own journey, I will carry with me the lessons of Parashat Va'era, and strive to live up to its message of courage, transformation, and perseverance.

FRIDA KAHLO WAS A MEXICAN ARTIST KNOWN FOR HER SELF-PORTRAITS THAT INCORPORATED ELEMENTS OF HER CULTURAL HERITAGE AND PERSONAL EXPERIENCES.

BO

Possible essay:

Parashat Bo is a rich and complex text that can be approached in many ways.

The narrative of Parashat Bo unfolds in a series of miracles and plagues that God visits upon the Egyptians in order to convince Pharaoh to release the Israelites from slavery. Through these events, the parsha explores the struggle between freedom and oppression, power and resistance, and faith and doubt.

As we read the verses and immerse ourselves in the world of the text, our minds wander and our imaginations soar. We hear the cries of the enslaved and the defiant, the triumphs of the righteous and the anguishes of the wicked, and the voices of the narrators and the characters. We also encounter many puzzles and paradoxes, such as the paradox of the hardening of Pharaoh's heart, which can be understood as both a divine action and a human choice.

But perhaps the most fascinating aspect of Parashat Bo is the way it represents the encounter between the infinite and the finite, the eternal and the temporal, the transcendent and the earthly. The plagues are not merely natural disasters, but also signs of divine power and purpose. They challenge our understanding of reality and question our assumptions about causality and morality.

Disrupting linearity and stability, Parashat Bo challenges our conventional perspectives and expectations. It invites us to delve into the multitudes of meanings and emotions that are latent in the text, and to uncover the depths of our own consciousness and spirituality.

In this way, Parashat Bo is like a labyrinthine river of thought and feeling that flows through the minds and hearts of the reader, the narrator, and the characters. It is a text that invites us to enter into its currents and be carried away by its currents, and to emerge transformed by the experience.

Parashat Bo is a reminder that language and narrative are not neutral or passive, but rather dynamic and creative forces that shape our perceptions and realities. It is a call to awaken to the richness and ambiguity of the words and worlds we inhabit, and to engage in the quest for meaning and truth with a sense of curiosity and wonder.

JAMES JOYCE WAS AN IRISH WRITER AND POET WHO IS CONSIDERED ONE OF THE MOST INFLUENTIAL MODERNIST WRITERS OF THE 20TH CENTURY.

IN THE STYLE OF SHEL SILVERSTEIN

Once upon a time, in Egypt land,
The Israelites were held in the grip of Pharaoh's hand,
But then came Moses, with a staff and a plea,
"Let my people go, and be set free!"

And so began the journey, with ten plagues in tow,
Each one worse than the last, and Pharaoh didn't know,
What to do or what to say, as he watched in despair,
His land and his power, slipping away.

And then came the final plague, the death of the firstborn,
And Pharaoh finally gave in, and the Israelites were gone,
Out of Egypt, and into the desert they roamed,
Following the pillars of cloud and fire, they were home.

And then came Parashat Bo, with its instructions clear,
The instructions for Passover, and the story to hear,
Of the salvation and the freedom, and the power of God,
And the people of Israel, and the journey they had.

So let us remember the story, and the journey we've made,
From Egypt to the Promised Land, and all that we've gained,
And let us celebrate with matzah, and wine and song,
The story of Passover, and the journey all year long!

SHEL SILVERSTEIN WAS AN AMERICAN POET, SINGER-SONGWRITER, CARTOONIST, AND CHILDREN'S AUTHOR KNOWN FOR HIS WITTY AND IMAGINATIVE WORKS, INCLUDING "THE GIVING TREE" AND "WHERE THE SIDEWALK ENDS."

IN THE STYLE OF JOB

Oh, the story of Parashat Bo, where do I begin? I remember the days when the Israelites lived in Egypt, oppressed and enslaved by Pharaoh. But then came the Lord's messenger, Moses, with the command to bring forth the people from their suffering. And yet, despite all the wonders and signs that were shown, Pharaoh's heart was hardened and he refused to let the Israelites go.

And so, the plagues descended upon Egypt, one after the other, each more devastating than the last. But still, Pharaoh's heart remained unyielding. And then came the final plague, the slaying of the firstborn, a dire warning of the Lord's power.

But what was the cost of Pharaoh's stubbornness? The cost was great, not only for the Egyptians but for the Israelites as well. For they too suffered, caught in the crossfire of Pharaoh's refusal to obey the Lord's command. And yet, in the midst of their suffering, the Israelites were given hope. For the Lord had promised to bring them to a land flowing with milk and honey, a land where they would be free from oppression and slavery.

And so, with their garments wrapped about them, they left Egypt in haste, following the pillar of cloud by day and the pillar of fire by night. But their journey was not without its trials and tribulations. They encountered hunger, thirst, and the fiery serpents in the wilderness. And yet, despite these hardships, they were sustained by the Lord's provisions and were led to the shores of the Red Sea.

And what was their fate when they reached the shores of the Red Sea? They were trapped, with Pharaoh's army in hot pursuit, their fate seemingly sealed. And yet, in their desperation, they cried out to the Lord, and God answered their call, dividing the sea and allowing them to cross over on dry ground.

But their journey was far from over. They encountered many more challenges and hardships, and yet the Lord was always there, guiding and sustaining them, leading them towards the land that God had promised them.

And so, as I reflect upon the story of Parashat Bo, I am reminded of the Lord's power and mercy, and of God's steadfast love for His people. For even in the midst of their trials and tribulations, He never forsook them, but sustained and protected them, leading them towards their ultimate destination.

Oh Lord, how great Thou art! Thy ways are not my ways, and Thy thoughts are not my thoughts. But I trust in Thee, for Thou art the Lord, the God of all creation, and I will sing Thy praises forevermore. Amen.

> *JOB, FOR WHOM A BOOK IN THE HEBREW BIBLE IS NAMED, WAS A WEALTHY AND RIGHTEOUS MAN WHO ENDURED TREMENDOUS SUFFERING, YET MAINTAINED HIS FAITH IN GOD THROUGH IT ALL.*

BESHALACH

In the style of Miriam the Prophetess

As I reflect on the events of Parashat Beshalach, my heart swells with pride and gratitude for the unwavering faith of my people. The journey from Egypt to the Promised Land was not easy, but with the guidance of Hashem and the leadership of Moses, we were able to overcome any obstacle that came our way.

The sight of the Red Sea splitting in two was a true testament to the power of Hashem, and the song of praise that we sang in response was a symbol of our faith and gratitude. I will never forget the feeling of hope and joy that filled my heart in that moment, knowing that Hashem was with us every step of the way.

As we continued on our journey, I was also reminded of the importance of following the commandments and laws given to us by Hashem. The manna that fell from heaven was a reminder of our dependence on Hashem and the need to follow God's laws and instructions in order to sustain our lives.

In these times of uncertainty and struggle, I am comforted by the events of Parashat Beshalach and the unwavering faith of my people. May we continue to follow the path set forth by Hashem and trust in God's guidance and protection. Amen.

> *Miriam the Prophetess was a powerful female leader and musician in ancient Israel, known for her prophetic gifts and role in leading the Israelites out of Egypt.*

Title: Beshalach - A Millerian Play

Characters:

Moses - A man who is the leader of the Israelites

Pharaoh - The ruler of Egypt

Aaron - Moses' brother and assistant

Miriam - Moses' sister and a prophetess

Scene: A plain stage with a wooden table in the center. Moses and Aaron are sitting at the table, Miriam enters.

Miriam: (Entering) Moses! Aaron! Pharaoh is coming!

Moses: (Getting up) What does he want this time?

Aaron: (Rising) I don't know, but we need to be ready for anything.

Miriam: (Looking outside) He's here, hurry!

Pharaoh enters.

Pharaoh: (Entering, speaking loudly) Moses! You will lead the Israelites back to Egypt or suffer the consequences!

Moses: (Stepping forward) Pharaoh, we have already been through this. The Lord has commanded us to leave Egypt and go to the Promised Land.

Pharaoh: (Angrily) I will not allow it!

Miriam: (Stepping forward) Pharaoh, do not underestimate the power of the Lord. He will protect us and provide for us, even in the midst of danger.

Pharaoh: (Scoffing) I have heard enough. I will send my army to stop you.

Moses: (Raising his hands) The Lord will part the sea and allow us to pass through safely.

Pharaoh: (Skeptical) We shall see.

Moses, Aaron, and Miriam exit as Pharaoh remains on stage, staring after them.

Pharaoh: (Alone) I will show them the power of Egypt. The Lord or no Lord, they will not escape me.

(End of play)

> *ARTHUR MILLER WAS AN AMERICAN PLAYWRIGHT AND ESSAYIST KNOWN FOR HIS CRITICALLY ACCLAIMED WORKS SUCH AS "DEATH OF A SALESMAN" AND "THE CRUCIBLE."*

IN THE STYLE OF RABBI JONATHAN SACKS

In Parashat Beshalach, we see the incredible story of the Children of Israel being freed from Egypt and the great miracles that accompany their journey through the desert. The central theme of this portion is that of faith and trust in God. The people are confronted with many challenges, including hunger, thirst, and the uncertainty of their future, but it is only through their unwavering faith in God that they are able to overcome these obstacles and reach their ultimate destination.

This parasha serves as a powerful reminder of the importance of faith in our own lives. Whether we are facing challenges or simply feeling lost and uncertain, we must always hold onto our faith in God and trust in God's plan for us. This can be difficult, especially when we are unable to see the end result, but it is only through our unwavering faith that we will be able to overcome the challenges we face and reach our own promised land.

Furthermore, Parashat Beshalach also highlights the crucial role that our leaders play in shaping our faith and guiding us towards our ultimate destiny. Moses, Aaron, and Miriam are all examples of leaders who serve as beacons of faith and inspire the people to trust in God. In our own lives, we must seek out leaders who embody these qualities and are able to guide us on our own spiritual journeys.

Parashat Beshalach is a powerful reminder of the importance of faith and trust in God, and of the role that our leaders play in shaping our faith. May we all strive to hold onto our faith in the face of adversity, and to seek out leaders who can guide us towards our own promised land.

> *RABBI JONATHAN SACKS WAS A RENOWNED BRITISH RABBI, PHILOSOPHER, AND AUTHOR WHO HAS SERVED AS THE CHIEF RABBI OF THE UNITED HEBREW CONGREGATIONS OF THE COMMONWEALTH FROM 1991 TO 2013.*

YITRO

Parashat Yitro, also known as Jethro, is a portion of the book of Exodus in the Hebrew Bible. It tells the story of Moses' encounter with his father-in-law Jethro and the subsequent revelation of the Ten Commandments on Mount Sinai. The narrative is rich in moral lessons and legal implications that are relevant even today.

One of the central themes of Parashat Yitro is the importance of delegation and the delegation of authority. Moses, who was leading the Israelites through the wilderness, was becoming overwhelmed with the demands of his role. Jethro, recognizing this, advised Moses to delegate some of his responsibilities to trusted leaders and to establish a system of courts to hear disputes and resolve legal problems. In my work "The Curse of Bigness," I also emphasized the importance of delegation and the decentralization of power. Excessive centralization of power in the hands of a few individuals or institutions is dangerous and prone to abuse. Smaller and more decentralized organizations are better suited to promote the public interest and prevent the concentration of power.

Another theme of Parashat Yitro is the concept of justice. The Ten Commandments, which were revealed to Moses on Mount Sinai, were not just religious or moral laws, but also laws of justice. They set forth basic principles of justice and fairness that were meant to govern the relationships between individuals and the community. In my work "What Publicity Can Do," I emphasized the importance of the public's right to know and the role of publicity in promoting justice and transparency. The free flow of information is essential to the preservation of democracy and the protection of individual rights.

Finally, Parashat Yitro is a reminder of the importance of self-reflection and humility. Moses, who was a great leader and teacher, was able to recognize his own limitations and to seek the advice of Jethro. Similarly, in my work "The Right to Privacy," I recognize the importance of humility in the face of power. Individuals have a right to privacy and that the state should not be allowed to invade this privacy without compelling reason. The state must always be subject to the scrutiny of the public and the public must have access to information about its activities.

In conclusion, Parashat Yitro is a rich and complex narrative that offers numerous lessons and insights relevant to contemporary society. We can see the importance of delegation and decentralization, the concept of justice, and the need for self-reflection and humility in the face of power.

These themes are as relevant today as they were thousands of years ago and serve as a reminder of the timeless wisdom of the Hebrew Bible.

> *Louis Brandeis was an American lawyer and Associate Justice of the Supreme Court, known for his advocacy for privacy rights and antitrust laws.*

In the style of Freddie Mercury

Verse 1:
Yitro came to Moshe's side
With advice he could not deny
Wise words for the chosen one
To lead his people, second to none

Chorus:
Yitro, Yitro, hear the call
With wisdom, you'll stand tall
From Midian to Sinai's height
A mentor to guide us through the night

Verse 2:
You saw the burden that he bore
A leader with so much more
Judgment for all the nation's cries
And with your words, he heard the prize

Chorus:
Yitro, Yitro, hear the call...

Bridge:
With his wise words, the laws were made
And with your guidance, we'll never stray
From the path of righteousness and might
With your help, we'll always shine so bright

Chorus:
Yitro, Yitro, hear the call...

Outro:
Yitro, Yitro, hear the call
With wisdom, you'll stand tall
From Midian to Sinai's height
A mentor to guide us through the night.

Freddie Mercury was a legendary singer, songwriter, and performer who rose to fame as the lead vocalist of the rock band Queen.

Dear friends,

I stand before you today to speak about Parashat Yitro and the power of love. The story of Yitro is one of great kindness, generosity and love, and it teaches us that love is not just a feeling, but it is a force that can change the world.

Yitro was a stranger, a priest of Midian, and yet he was welcomed into the camp of the Israelites with open arms. He saw the suffering of the people, the endless work of Moses, and he knew that something had to change. He came with a solution, to create a system of judges, to help alleviate the burden of Moses, and in doing so, he demonstrated the true power of love.

Love is not just an emotion, it is a way of life. It is a choice to be kind, to be patient, to be compassionate, even when we may not feel like it. Yitro's love was demonstrated in his actions, in his willingness to help those who were not his own people, but whom he saw as brothers and sisters in need.

Like Yitro, we can all make a difference in the lives of others through our actions. Love can be shown through simple acts of kindness, through offering a helping hand, or even through listening to someone when they need someone to talk to.

As I once said, "Love is like a river, constantly flowing, giving life to everything it touches." This is the true power of love, its ability to give life, to heal, and to bring people together.

In the words of Yitro, "This is a great thing that you are doing."[10] We can all take part in this great thing, by showing love and compassion in our daily lives, by treating others with kindness and respect, and by recognizing that we are all in this together.

---

[10] Though I've largely refrained from commenting on the ChatGPT texts, this purported quote demonstrates the limitations of the technology and therefore warrants our attention. Yitro does not say this in the text at all. In fact, this is the JPS translation of the Hebrew: "*But Moses' father-in-law said to him, 'The thing you are doing is **not** right; you will surely wear yourself out, and these people as well. For the task is too heavy for you; you cannot do it alone.'* (Ex. 18:17-18)" Somehow, the AI conflated the gift of Yitro's presence (true) with Yitro's approval of Moses' method of judging (not true), woven in a clever way with Maya Angelou's teachings about love. Clearly, there is not only a lack of depth in ChatGPT's expression, but error in its understanding.

So let us learn from Yitro, let us embrace the power of love, and let us work to make this world a better place for all.

With love and respect,

Maya Angelou

> *Maya Angelou was a legendary poet, author, and civil rights activist who inspired millions through her powerful writing and outspoken activism.*

MISHPATIM

As the ruler of ancient Babylon, I, understand the importance of law and order in maintaining a just and prosperous society. This is why I am proud to share my thoughts on Parashat Mishpatim, a section of the Torah that outlines laws and commandments for the Israelites.

Just as I did in my own Code of Hammurabi, Parashat Mishpatim emphasizes the power of law in creating a harmonious community. The laws outlined in this portion of the Torah range from civil matters, such as debt and property rights, to moral and ethical guidelines, such as treating slaves with respect and honoring one's parents.

What sets these laws apart is their basis in fairness and equality. Parashat Mishpatim clearly states that the laws apply to all members of the community, regardless of their status or wealth. This is crucial in creating a society where all individuals are treated with dignity and respect, and where justice is upheld.

Moreover, the laws in Parashat Mishpatim are not simply a list of rules to be followed. They serve as a moral compass for the Israelites, guiding them towards a righteous and just way of life. The laws serve as a reminder that individuals are not only responsible for their own actions, but also for how they treat others.

In the same way that my own code served as a model for other civilizations, Parashat Mishpatim continues to be a source of inspiration for those seeking to create a just society. Its laws serve as a testament to the power of law in promoting equality, fairness, and justice.

Mishpatim is a powerful reminder of the importance of law in shaping society. It serves as a model for those seeking to create a harmonious and just community, where individuals are treated with dignity and respect and where justice is upheld. May we always be guided by the principles outlined in this portion of the Torah, as we strive towards a better and more just world.

Hammurabi was a Babylonian king and the author of one of the first known sets of laws in human history.

As a woman who dedicated her life to the fight for workers' rights, I cannot help but reflect on the teachings of this week's Parashat Mishpatim and their significance for laborers everywhere.

In this portion of the Torah, God commands the Israelites to follow various laws and regulations, including rules for fair labor practices. This is a clear message that even in ancient times, the importance of fair labor was recognized and valued by God.

However, this message has not always been upheld throughout history. The exploitation of workers has been a pervasive issue, and still exists today in many industries. Sweatshops and child labor are just two examples of the injustices that workers face, both here in America and abroad.

As a young woman, I was horrified by the conditions in the garment factories where I worked. I was paid low wages, forced to work long hours, and subjected to unsafe working conditions. I realized that I was not alone in my struggles, and I knew that something had to be done to improve the lives of workers.

This is why I became an activist, joining the International Ladies' Garment Workers' Union (ILGWU) and leading the "Uprising of the 20,000," a strike of Jewish and Italian immigrant women in the New York garment industry. I fought for better wages, shorter work hours, and safe working conditions, and we achieved many of these goals through our efforts.

As we read Parashat Mishpatim, we must remember the lessons of fair labor practices and stand in solidarity with workers everywhere. The Torah teaches us that workers have inherent value and deserve to be treated with dignity and respect. We must work to ensure that these values are upheld and that workers are not exploited for the benefit of corporations and wealthy individuals.

Let us continue the fight for fair labor and stand up for the rights of workers everywhere.

Clara Lemlich was a Ukrainian-American labor activist and leader of the Uprising of 20,000, a seminal moment in the history of the garment workers' union movement.

In the style of John Jay

Parashat Mishpatim is a section of the Torah that outlines laws and regulations that guide the behavior of the Jewish people. In this section, we see the power of law as a force that shapes the society and ensures that justice is served. The law is the cornerstone of a free society and the source of justice.

In Parashat Mishpatim, we see that the laws and regulations are meant to protect the rights of individuals and ensure that justice is served. For example, the laws relating to property rights and theft serve to protect the rights of property owners and ensure that those who violate those rights are punished. Similarly, laws relating to debt and contracts serve to protect the rights of creditors and ensure that debtors fulfill their obligations.

The power of law is also evident in the way that it serves as a deterrent to crime. When laws are well-known and widely understood, people are less likely to engage in criminal activities, knowing that there will be consequences if they do. This creates a safer and more secure society, where everyone can live and work without fear of being exploited or oppressed.

Moreover, the power of law is seen in the way that it promotes fairness and equality. By setting out clear rules and regulations, everyone is treated equally and there is no room for bias or discrimination. This is especially important in a society that values justice, as it ensures that everyone is held to the same standard, regardless of their background, wealth, or status.

In conclusion, Parashat Mishpatim serves as a reminder of the power of law and its role in shaping society. The laws outlined in Parashat Mishpatim serve to protect the rights of individuals, deter crime, and promote fairness and equality. These values are timeless and continue to be relevant today, as we strive to create a society that is just and equitable for all.

> *John Jay was a statesman, lawyer, and one of the founding fathers of the United States, serving as the first Chief Justice of the Supreme Court and co-authoring the Federalist Papers.*

TERUMAH

Parashat Terumah speaks to the importance of community and the role of individual contributions in building a shared space. As we read the verses, we are reminded of the power of collective action and the responsibility we have to one another.

In Terumah, the Israelites are commanded to build a Mishkan, or Tabernacle, as a dwelling place for God in their midst. The Mishkan was to be constructed from the donations of the community, with each person contributing materials and resources according to their means. This act of giving was not just about the physical building of the Mishkan, but about the formation of a community bonded by shared purpose and responsibility.

Similarly, in our own lives and communities, it is through the contributions of each individual that we build and sustain the spaces and institutions that matter to us. Whether it be through volunteering, donating resources, or simply offering support and encouragement, it is through our combined efforts that we are able to achieve great things.

Throughout my career, I fought tirelessly to dismantle systemic barriers to equality and to ensure that everyone had access to the protections and opportunities afforded by the law. I understood that the advancement of individual rights was inextricably linked to the health and vitality of the community as a whole.

Just as the Mishkan was built through the collective efforts of the Israelites, so too are our communities and institutions strengthened by the contributions of each individual. In words I've written elsewhere, "Real change, enduring change, happens one step at a time."

In Terumah, we are taught that our obligations to one another and to the greater community extend beyond simply meeting our own needs. Each of us has a role to play in building and sustaining the spaces and institutions that matter to us, and it is through our combined efforts that we are able to achieve true change and progress.

As we reflect on the lessons of Parashat Terumah, let us be inspired to redouble our efforts to build strong, inclusive, and equitable communities. For only through the contributions of each individual, can we build a world that is truly worthy.

Ruth Bader Ginsburg was an Associate Justice of the Supreme Court of the United States and a champion of gender equality and civil rights.

I firmly believe in the importance of taxation in a thriving society. In this regard, parashat terumah, the portion of the Torah that outlines the construction of the Tabernacle and the collection of materials for its creation, serves as an example of the power of taxation in supporting public endeavors.

The Tabernacle, as described in parashat terumah, was a magnificent structure that required a significant amount of resources and materials to build. The Israelites were called upon to contribute their own wealth, including gold, silver, and other precious materials, to support the construction of this sacred space.

This act of giving reflects the importance of taxation in supporting public works and initiatives. In a similar manner, our government relies on taxes to fund the building and maintenance of public structures and institutions, such as roads, schools, and hospitals. These facilities serve as the backbone of our society, providing essential services to all citizens.

In the case of parashat terumah, the contribution of materials was not only a matter of obligation, but also an act of faith and devotion. The Israelites believed in the importance of the Tabernacle, and they were willing to sacrifice their own wealth to support its construction. This same principle applies to our government and the taxes we pay. We must trust that the government is using our tax dollars wisely, to support initiatives that will improve our society and the lives of our citizens.

Moreover, taxation can also help to ensure that wealth is distributed fairly in a society. In parashat terumah, all members of the Israelite community were called upon to contribute, regardless of their wealth. This act of equality ensured that the burden of supporting the Tabernacle was shared by all members of the community.

Similarly, in our society, a progressive tax system is designed to ensure that those who are wealthier pay a larger portion of their income in taxes. This helps to ensure that the costs of supporting public initiatives are shared fairly, and that the burden does not fall on those who are struggling to make ends meet.

Terumah provides us with a powerful example of the importance of taxation in supporting public initiatives. Through the act of giving, we can support the construction of structures that serve the common good, while also ensuring that wealth is distributed fairly. As a founding father of this great nation, I strongly believe that taxes are a necessary tool for building a thriving society, and I encourage all citizens to view them in a positive light, as a means of supporting the common good.

Alexander Hamilton was a statesman, military leader, and one of the Founding Fathers of the United States who played a key role in establishing the nation's economic system.

As an architect and designer, I have always been fascinated by the concept of building and construction. This is why parashat Terumah, or the portion of the Torah that describes the building of the Tabernacle, holds a special place in my heart. It speaks to the importance of not just constructing physical structures, but also the spiritual ones that exist within us.

In this portion of the Torah, God commands Moses to collect offerings from the people of Israel in order to build the Tabernacle. This act of giving is not just a financial transaction, but a spiritual one as well. The people of Israel are being asked to give of their wealth in order to build a sacred space where they can connect with God.

This act of giving is similar to the concept of taxation. In our modern world, we pay taxes to support the physical structures and institutions that make our society function. In the same way, the Israelites were asked to give their wealth to support the building of a spiritual institution that would sustain their faith and community.

The act of giving in Parashat Terumah is not just about the financial transaction. It is about the act of sacrifice. The people of Israel are being asked to give their most valuable possessions, their wealth, in order to build something greater than themselves. This sacrifice is what makes the act of giving so powerful. It is a reminder that we are all part of a larger community and that we have a responsibility to contribute to the betterment of that community.

As a designer, I see the act of giving as an opportunity to create something beautiful and meaningful. The Tabernacle, as described in Parashat Terumah, was a magnificent structure, built with the finest materials and designed with intricate details. It was a testament to the skill and creativity of the Israelites and a symbol of their devotion to God.

In the same way, the buildings and structures we build today can be beautiful and meaningful. They can reflect our values, our history, and our aspirations. Whether it is through the use of natural materials, attention to detail, or a focus on sustainability, we can create buildings that inspire and uplift those who use them.

In conclusion, Parashat Terumah and the concept of taxation both speak to the importance of giving and sacrifice. They remind us that we are all part of a larger community and that we have a responsibility to contribute to the betterment of that community. As a designer, I see this as an opportunity to create something beautiful and meaningful, a testament to our skill and creativity and a symbol of our devotion to the greater good.

> *Frank Lloyd Wright was an American architect and interior designer who revolutionized the design of modern buildings with his organic, holistic approach.*

TETZAVEH

In the style of Mr. Rogers

Dear friends,

I hope you are all doing well today. I wanted to talk to you about a topic that is very important to me, and that is the idea of being a good neighbor. This week, we are reading Parshat Tetzaveh, which is all about the idea of being a good leader, and the responsibilities that come along with that. But I believe that being a good leader starts with being a good neighbor.

When I was growing up, my mother always taught me the importance of treating others with kindness and respect. She would say, "Always treat others the way you want to be treated." I believe this is the core of what it means to be a good neighbor. We must all strive to be kind, understanding, and compassionate towards those around us, regardless of our differences.

In Parshat Tetzaveh, we are reminded of the importance of serving others, and the role of the Kohen Gadol, or the High Priest, in leading the people. The High Priest was responsible for representing the people before God, and ensuring that the community was living in a way that was pleasing to God. But I believe that this goes beyond just the High Priest, and extends to all of us as individuals.

We are all called to be leaders in our own way, and to serve our communities by being good neighbors. This means taking care of each other, helping each other, and being there for each other in times of need. It means listening to each other, supporting each other, and being kind to each other, even when we may not agree on everything.

In conclusion, being a good neighbor is at the heart of what it means to be a good leader. When we show kindness, compassion, and understanding towards those around us, we create a community that is strong and supportive. Let us all strive to be good neighbors, and to lead by example in all that we do.

Won't you be my neighbor?

Warmly,
Mr. Rogers

Mr. Rogers was a beloved television personality known for his warm and nurturing demeanor as host of the educational children's show "Mister Rogers' Neighborhood."

In the Style of Diane von Furstenberg

As a fashion designer and CEO of my own brand, I have always been fascinated by the beauty of design and the art of dressing. And, this week's Parashat Tetzaveh, which focuses on the design of the Tabernacle, has given me even more reason to reflect on the importance of design in our lives.

The Tabernacle was a complex structure built by the Israelites as a place for God to dwell among them. The design of the Tabernacle was not just functional but also beautiful and aesthetically pleasing. Each piece of clothing, each garment, each lamp, and every piece of furniture was designed to perfection with intricate details and patterns.

Just as the Tabernacle was designed to be both functional and beautiful, so too, is fashion design. Fashion is not just about covering our bodies but also about expressing ourselves and creating a visual statement. A designer's role is to create pieces that are not only practical but also aesthetically pleasing.

Similarly, fashion design and the Tabernacle share the idea of symbolism. The Tabernacle was designed to symbolize God's presence among the Israelites. And, in fashion, designers use symbols to communicate ideas and emotions. For example, I have always been inspired by the Greek goddesses and the power they represented. So, I often use the symbol of the wrap dress to represent the empowering feeling of being in control of one's own life.

In conclusion, parashat Tetzaveh reminds us of the importance of design in our lives. Whether it's designing a piece of clothing or a structure, the principles of functionality, beauty, and symbolism remain the same. As a fashion designer, I believe that design has the power to impact our lives in a positive way and that we should always strive to create pieces that are both practical and beautiful.

> *Diane von Fürstenberg was a fashion designer and businesswoman known for creating the iconic wrap dress. Born in Belgium to a Jewish family, she survived the Holocaust and went on to build a successful fashion empire.*

IN THE STYLE OF NORMAN MAILER

Ladies and Gentlemen,

Allow me to address you today on a topic that is both fascinating and thought-provoking: Parashat Tetzaveh and the power of imagination. I believe that imagination is one of the most valuable gifts that we possess as human beings. It allows us to go beyond the constraints of the present, to envision new possibilities, and to see things in a different light.

Parashat Tetzaveh is one of the weekly portions in the book of Exodus, and it focuses on the instructions given to Moses for the consecration of the Tabernacle and the garments of the priests. The portion is rich in symbolic language and imagery, and it offers us a glimpse into the ancient Jewish imagination. In this passage, we see how the Israelites were able to use their imagination to create a powerful and sacred space, one that would serve as a focal point for their religious and cultural identity.

But what does this have to do with our modern world, you might ask? Well, I believe that the imagination is just as important today as it was thousands of years ago. In a world that is increasingly complex and challenging, it is easy to get lost in the day-to-day struggles and to forget the power of our own imagination. However, if we can tap into it, we can unlock new possibilities and find new ways of seeing the world around us.

One of the things that I admire about Parashat Tetzaveh is the way in which it encourages us to use our imagination. The instructions given to Moses are filled with vivid descriptions of the colors, materials, and design of the Tabernacle and the priests' garments. These descriptions are meant to stimulate our imagination, to help us visualize the beauty and majesty of the Tabernacle. By doing so, they invite us to participate in the creation of this sacred space, to use our own imagination to bring it to life.

In conclusion, I would like to emphasize that the power of imagination is not limited to ancient times or religious texts. It is a gift that we all possess, and it is up to us to use it to create a better world. Whether we are building a religious temple, a work of art, or simply exploring new ideas, our imagination is the key that unlocks the doors of our potential. So, let us embrace it, nurture it, and use it to make a positive difference in the world. Thank you.

> *Norman Mailer was an American novelist, journalist, and cultural commentator known for his bold and controversial writing style. He won two Pulitzer Prizes for his works and was considered one of the most influential writers of the 20th century.*

KI TISSA

In the Style of Sigmund Freud

Parashat Ki Tissa is a portion of the Torah that recounts the story of the golden calf and Moses' descent from Mount Sinai with the tablets of the law. In this story, the Israelites, frustrated by Moses' prolonged absence, demand that Aaron, his brother, create a deity for them to worship. Aaron complies and crafts a golden calf, which the Israelites then worship as their God. When Moses returns, he is angry and shattered by the sight of the idol, which he destroys and demands that the people repent.

We can understand this story as an expression of fear and the search for security in the face of uncertainty. The Israelites are afraid because Moses, their leader, has been gone for a long time, and they are uncertain about what will happen to them. They crave stability and comfort, and so they turn to the creation of a deity to provide them with the security and assurance they desire.

From a psychoanalytic perspective, the golden calf represents a manifestation of the collective unconscious of the Israelites. This unconscious is a store of inherited knowledge, experiences, and feelings that are shared by all members of a group. The golden calf serves as a symbol of the unconscious desires and fears of the Israelites, which have been projected onto the idol as a means of coping with the uncertainty and fear that they feel.

Furthermore, Freud's theory of the death drive can also be applied to this story. According to Freud, the death drive is the unconscious urge to return to a state of inactivity, death, or nothingness. In the case of the golden calf, the death drive can be seen as the desire to return to a state of security and comfort, even if that means giving up one's own autonomy and independence. By worshiping the golden calf, the Israelites are sacrificing their own individual identity and surrendering their will to the idol, which serves as a symbol of the death drive.

In conclusion, Parashat Ki Tissa can be interpreted through the lens of my theories of the unconscious and the death drive. The story of the golden calf represents the Israelites' fear and search for security in the face of uncertainty, which leads to the manifestation of the collective unconscious and the surrender of their individuality to the death drive. This interpretation highlights the enduring relevance of the Torah and its ability to provide insight into the human condition and the universal themes of fear, security, and identity.

Sigmund Freud was an Austrian neurologist and the founder of psychoanalysis.

In the style of Matsuo Bashō

Golden calf born,
Israelite's hearts filled with sin,
Moses' rage unfolds.

God's glory descends,
Tables of stone receive the law,
Moses' face shines bright.

Anoint Aaron,
Levite's to be priests, divine,
Israel's redemption.

Sabbath holy day,
Sign of God's creation rest,
Covenant fulfilled.

Golden jewelry,
Donations for Tabernacle,
God's presence felt near.

The Ark completed,
Moses covers it with veil,
Glory rests within.

Cloud of God's presence,
Leads Israelites in their journey,
Promised land ahead.

Matsuo Bashō was a Japanese haiku poet and wanderer who lived during the late 17th century. He is widely regarded as one of the greatest haiku poets of all time and his works are considered a cornerstone of the Japanese literary tradition.

Parashat Ki Tissa is rich in symbolism and allegory. In order to fully appreciate the depth and complexity of this text, it is important to understand the literary style and cultural context of the time.

The literary style of the biblical period as a combination of story-telling and legal code. Ki Tissa is a prime example of this style, as it interweaves a narrative of the Israelites' worship of the Golden Calf with the laws of the Mishkan (Tabernacle) and the consecration of the priesthood.

One of the most prominent symbols in the parashah is the Golden Calf itself. The calf represents the Israelites' temptation to worship false gods and their abandonment of the God who delivered them from slavery in Egypt. The episode serves as a cautionary tale about the dangers of idol worship and the importance of staying true to the divine commandments.

The construction of the Mishkan and the consecration of the priesthood serve as another layer of symbolism in the parashah. The Mishkan represents God's presence among the people, while the priesthood represents the mediators between God and the Israelites. The consecration of the priesthood symbolizes the Israelites' acceptance of God's rule and the beginning of a new era of obedience and devotion.

Another powerful symbol in the parashah is the commandment to keep the Sabbath holy. The Sabbath symbolizes the Jewish people's rest and reflection, as well as their commitment to God. By keeping the Sabbath, the Israelites are reminded of their divine origins and the blessings they have received from God.

In conclusion, Ki Tissa is a rich and multi-layered text, full of symbolism and allegory. By understanding the literary style and cultural context of the time, one can gain a deeper appreciation for the depth and complexity of this text, and the lessons it holds for the Jewish people.

JACOB NEUSNER WAS AN AMERICAN SCHOLAR AND RABBI WHO WAS A LEADING FIGURE IN THE ACADEMIC STUDY OF JUDAISM AND RELIGION.

VAYAKHEL

Parashat Vayakhel tells the story of the building of the Tabernacle in the wilderness. This event is significant not only because it marked a turning point in the history of the Jewish people, but also because it reveals much about the nature of gratitude and the role it plays in our lives.

Gratitude is a complex emotion that encompasses many different facets of human experience. It encompasses a feeling of thankful recognition for what we have received, as well as a recognition of the role that others have played in our lives. In this sense, gratitude is not simply a feeling, but a way of looking at the world and at our place in it.

The building of the Tabernacle was a massive undertaking that involved the entire community of the Jewish people. Each person was asked to contribute according to their ability, and the result was a magnificent structure that symbolized their unity and shared purpose. This act of giving and receiving, of working together for a common goal, was the foundation of the community's gratitude.

In the same way, gratitude is not simply a matter of feeling thankful, but of acting on that gratitude by giving back to others. Whether it is through acts of kindness, volunteering, or simply sharing our time and resources, it is through giving that we express our gratitude for all that we have received.

But what is it about gratitude that makes it such a powerful and transformative emotion? I believe that it is rooted in the recognition of the interconnectedness of all things. When we are grateful, we recognize that we are not alone in the world, but are part of a larger whole. We see that our success and happiness are not just a result of our own efforts, but are also the result of the efforts of others.

This sense of interconnectedness, of being part of something greater than ourselves, is what makes gratitude so profound. It is not just a feeling, but a way of seeing the world and our place in it. It is a recognition of the fact that we are all connected, and that our lives are intertwined in ways that are often beyond our understanding.

In conclusion, Parashat Vayakhel and the building of the Tabernacle serve as a reminder of the importance of gratitude in our lives. Whether it is through acts of giving and receiving, or through a recognition of the interconnectedness of all things, gratitude is a powerful and transformative emotion that can help us to see the world in a new and more positive light.

Just as the Tabernacle was built through the collective efforts of the Jewish people, so too can we build a world that is filled with gratitude and compassion by working together and recognizing the role that others play in our lives.

Oliver Sacks was a renowned British neurologist and author who explored the workings of the human mind in his many books and essays.

In the style of Henrietta Szold

The Jewish people's return to their homeland was a necessary step towards reclaiming their heritage and creating a better future for themselves. As I wrote in my essay, "The Jewish Problem and Its Solution," the Jewish people needed a place of their own, where they could build a society based on their own values, traditions, and culture. This ideal of a Jewish homeland was the foundation of my support for Zionism, the movement to establish a Jewish state in Palestine.

In many ways, Parashat Vayakhel, which recounts the building of the Tabernacle in the desert, can be seen as a parallel to the Zionist ideal of creating a new home for the Jewish people. In the story, the Jewish people are commanded by God to build a sacred space, where they can gather and worship. Just as the Tabernacle was a symbol of the Jewish people's connection to their God, the Jewish homeland in Palestine would serve as a symbol of the Jewish people's connection to their history, traditions, and culture.

The establishment of a Jewish state in Palestine as a way for the Jewish people to reclaim their identity and heritage, which had been lost or diminished during centuries of exile and oppression. The Jewish people needed a place of their own, where they could rebuild their community, rekindle their traditions, and create a society that reflected their values and aspirations.

In this sense, Zionism was rooted in the idea of creating a new kind of Jewish society, one that would be based on equality, social justice, and cultural richness. I believed that the Jewish people could only truly flourish in a place where they had complete control over their own lives and destiny, free from the constraints of foreign rule or the fear of persecution.

Like the Tabernacle in Parashat Vayakhel, the Jewish homeland in Palestine would be a symbol of hope, resilience, and renewal. It would demonstrate the Jewish people's determination to survive and thrive, even in the face of adversity. And it would serve as a testament to the Jewish people's connection to their God, their history, and their heritage.

In conclusion, Parashat Vayakhel and the ideal of Zionism were deeply intertwined in my vision of the future. Both reflected the belief that the Jewish people needed a place of their own, where they could reclaim their heritage and create a better future for themselves.

Henrietta Szold was a Jewish American educator and humanitarian who founded the Hadassah Women's Zionist Organization of America.

I would like to compare the Mishkan in Parashat Vayakhel and the Jerusalem Temple, both of which have held great significance in our history and religion.

The Mishkan, built in the desert as a portable dwelling for the Lord, was a symbol of the Israelites' obedience and devotion to God. Its construction was a collective effort, with each member of the community contributing their skills and resources. The Mishkan was a simple yet elegant structure, built with a combination of natural materials and divine inspiration.

On the other hand, the Jerusalem Temple, which I had the privilege of building, was a magnificent and grand structure, made of the finest materials and adorned with gold and precious stones. It represented the prosperity and power of our kingdom and the central role of God in our lives. The Temple was a place of worship and sacrifice, where the people of Israel could come to offer their prayers and offerings to the Lord.

Both the Mishkan and the Temple were significant not only for their physical beauty but also for the spiritual connection they provided between the people of Israel and God. They both served as a reminder of the covenant between God and God's people, and their presence was a symbol of God's presence among us.

In conclusion, both the Mishkan and the Jerusalem Temple played an important role in our history and religion, each with its unique significance and purpose. They were both expressions of our devotion and love for God and served as a reminder of his presence in our lives.

KING SOLOMON WAS A LEGENDARY RULER OF ANCIENT ISRAEL KNOWN FOR HIS WISDOM, WEALTH, AND BUILDING OF THE TEMPLE IN JERUSALEM.

PEKUDEI

In the style of Dylan Thomas

With hammer and chisel, they built the Ark
A sacred symbol, with great care and pride
Inscribed with the Name, so the world would mark

In Pekudei, we read of their work
Detailed accounts of gold and blue
With hammer and chisel, they built the Ark

Moses, their leader, heard God's murmur
Instructions for the tabernacle true
Inscribed with the Name, so the world would mark

And when their labor was complete, a perk
God's presence filled the space anew
With hammer and chisel, they built the Ark

From silver and bronze, they made the parts
Their hearts and hands in harmony, true
Inscribed with the Name, so the world would mark

We honor their art, with grateful heart
For the Ark that still shines bright and true
With hammer and chisel, they built the Ark
Inscribed with the Name, so the world would mark.

Dylan Thomas was a Welsh poet and playwright known for his imaginative, lyrical, and emotive writing style.

IN THE STYLE OF LILY SAFRA

Parashat Pekudei is one of the most significant portions in the book of Exodus, detailing the completion of the construction of the Tabernacle. As a philanthropist and patron of Jewish education and heritage, the teachings of this parasha held a special place in my heart.

The Tabernacle was a place of worship for the Israelites, a symbol of their connection to God and a representation of God's presence among them. The construction of the Tabernacle was a meticulous process, involving a team of skilled craftsmen and detailed instructions from God himself. It was an act of devotion and obedience, a demonstration of the Israelites' commitment to their faith.

In Parashat Pekudei, we learn about the final stages of the Tabernacle's construction, including the creation of the Ark of the Covenant, the Menorah, and the curtains. The Israelites' dedication to their God is evident in their tireless efforts to create a fitting home for God's presence. It is a reminder of the importance of building meaningful connections with our faith, of putting in the time and effort to deepen our understanding and relationship with God.

As a philanthropist, I had the privilege of supporting initiatives that promote Jewish education and heritage. I believed that it is our duty to pass down the teachings and traditions of our faith to future generations, to help them establish their own connections to God and their heritage. The Tabernacle, with its intricate construction and symbolism, is a perfect example of the value of preserving and sharing our cultural and spiritual legacy.

Parashat Pekudei teaches us about the significance of devotion and obedience in our relationship with God. It reminds us of the importance of preserving our heritage and passing down its teachings to future generations. As we continue to support Jewish education and heritage initiatives, let us strive to embody the spirit of the Israelites, who dedicated themselves to the creation of a fitting home for God's presence.

LILY SAFRA, A JEWISH PHILANTHROPIST, DEDICATED HER LIFE TO SUPPORTING VARIOUS CHARITABLE CAUSES AND PRESERVING JEWISH HERITAGE.

In the style of Eeyore

As I lay in my gloomy corner of the Hundred Acre Wood, I couldn't help but reflect on this week's parashah. As a pessimistic and cynical donkey, I often find myself feeling disheartened by the events that unfold in my life.

Parashat Pekudei speaks of the meticulous accounting of the materials and resources used to build the Tabernacle. I must say, this attention to detail and accounting is something that I can appreciate. In my own life, I often find that things don't go according to plan and I'm left feeling frustrated and discouraged. However, just as the Israelites carefully counted and accounted for every item used in building the Tabernacle, I too must be mindful of the resources I have and be careful in how I use them.

I also found comfort in the idea that every single detail in the construction of the Tabernacle was carefully planned and executed according to God's instructions. Despite the obstacles and challenges they faced, the Israelites did not give up and instead, they continued to work diligently and follow God's plan. This serves as a reminder that even in the darkest of times, I too must have faith and trust that there is a plan for me, and that I must continue to work towards it despite any setbacks or challenges I may encounter.

In conclusion, Pekudei has taught me the importance of being mindful of my resources and to have faith and trust in a higher plan. While I may still have my pessimistic moments, I know that I must work towards building a better future for myself, just as the Israelites worked towards building the Tabernacle.

> *Eeyore is a lovable and melancholic donkey who is best known for his pessimistic outlook on life. Despite his downbeat demeanor, Eeyore has a warm and gentle heart, making him one of the most beloved characters in the Winnie the Pooh universe.*

LEVITICUS/VAYIKRA

Leviticus, Societal Justice, and Love

IN THE STYLE OF RABBI MENACHEM CREDITOR

Leviticus is one of the most important books in the Jewish Bible, and it provides a comprehensive framework for understanding societal justice and love within the context of Jewish tradition. This essay will explore the themes of Leviticus, specifically, how it teaches us about the importance of societal justice and love in our lives.

At the heart of Leviticus is the idea of holiness, or kedushah. The book teaches that everything in the world can be holy if it is used in the right way. This includes the land, the animals, and even people. Leviticus emphasizes the importance of treating each other with kindness and compassion, and it provides a detailed set of laws and rituals for achieving this goal.

One of the most important themes in Leviticus is the idea of societal justice. The book emphasizes the importance of treating everyone in society with fairness and equality, regardless of their status or background. Leviticus provides laws for how to treat the poor, the stranger, and the foreigner, emphasizing the importance of not oppressing those who are vulnerable. In Leviticus 19:18, it says, "You shall not take vengeance or bear a grudge against any of your people, but you shall love your neighbor as yourself: I am the Lord." This verse emphasizes the importance of treating others with love and compassion, rather than seeking revenge or holding grudges.

Another important theme in Leviticus is the idea of love. Leviticus teaches that love is not just an emotion, but an action. Leviticus 19:34 says, "The stranger who resides with you shall be to you as one of your citizens; you shall love him as yourself, for you were strangers in the land of Egypt: I am the Lord your God." This verse emphasizes the importance of showing love and compassion to those who are different from us. Leviticus also provides a detailed set of laws for how to show love to others, including providing for the poor, caring for the sick, and forgiving those who have wronged us.

In addition to its emphasis on societal justice and love, Leviticus also teaches us about the importance of ritual and tradition in Jewish life. The book provides detailed instructions for how to observe the various festivals and holy days, emphasizing the importance of these rituals in maintaining a strong sense of community and connection to God.

Overall, Leviticus teaches us that the key to living a fulfilling and meaningful life is to treat others with kindness, compassion, and love. The book provides a comprehensive framework for achieving these goals, emphasizing the importance of societal justice, ritual, and tradition in Jewish life. Leviticus teaches us that we must be constantly striving to create a more just and loving society, and that this requires a deep commitment to our community, our tradition, and our relationship with God.

VAYIKRA

IN THE STYLE OF JACOB MILGROM

In Parshat Vayikra, we see the Lord calling out to Moses and speaking to him from the Tent of Meeting, instructing him on the laws of the sacrifices. These sacrifices, ranging from burnt offerings to peace offerings, serve as a means of atonement and a way for the Israelites to draw close to the Lord. However, what truly stands out in this portion is the emphasis placed on love, the overarching theme of the Book of Vayikra. The sacrifices serve as a physical manifestation of this love, as the Israelites are offering up a portion of their possessions to the Lord.

But what makes Vayikra so unique is the Lord's own demonstration of love towards the Israelites. Despite their repeated transgressions, the Lord remains steadfast in his love for them, accepting their offerings and providing a way for them to seek atonement. This serves as a powerful reminder that true love is not dependent on the actions of others, but rather is unconditional and unwavering.

Furthermore, the love commanded in Vayikra is not just a passive emotion, but rather an active force in the lives of the Israelites. The sacrifices they bring are not just symbols of their love, but actual acts of love in and of themselves. In this way, the Lord is teaching the Israelites how to live a life of love, not just towards him, but towards one another as well.

In conclusion, Parshat Vayikra serves as a beautiful reminder of the power and importance of love. Through the Lord's demonstration of love towards the Israelites and the commands for them to love him and one another, we are reminded of the transformative impact that love can have in our lives. May we learn from this portion and strive to live a life of love, both towards the Lord and towards those around us.

JACOB MILGROM (1923-2010) WAS AN AMERICAN BIBLICAL SCHOLAR AND PROFESSOR OF JEWISH STUDIES, BEST KNOWN FOR HIS INFLUENTIAL WORKS ON THE BIBLICAL BOOK OF LEVITICUS AND THE PRIESTHOOD IN ANCIENT ISRAEL. HIS WRITINGS ON THE SUBJECT HAVE BEEN CONSIDERED GROUNDBREAKING IN THEIR EXPLORATION OF THE SOCIAL AND HISTORICAL CONTEXT OF THE BOOK.

As we delve into Parashat Vayikra and the Book of Leviticus, we are confronted with the central theme of sacrifice and the role it plays in our relationship with God. This theme is not just a physical act, but a spiritual one as well.

Leviticus is often referred to as the "book of sacrifice", but it is much more than that. She would say that the act of sacrifice is not only about offering a physical item to God, but about making a spiritual offering as well. Through sacrifice, we are symbolically surrendering our ego, our desires, and our sense of control, and surrendering it to God.

The sacrifices in Leviticus are not only about making an offering to God, but about making an offering of ourselves. The purpose of sacrifice is to draw closer to God and to allow God to be the center of our lives. By offering ourselves to God, we are able to focus on the things that truly matter, rather than the things that distract us.

Furthermore, the sacrifice described in Leviticus is not just about the physical act, but about the state of mind in which we make the offering. It is not enough to simply offer a physical item to God, but we must also offer our hearts, our minds, and our souls. This requires us to have a state of mind that is focused on God, and to surrender ourselves to God's will.

In conclusion, the Book of Leviticus is not just about sacrifice, but about the spiritual act of surrendering ourselves to God. The sacrifices described in Leviticus are not just physical acts, but spiritual ones as well. By offering ourselves to God, we are able to focus on the things that truly matter, rather than the things that distract us, and we are able to draw closer to God.

NECHAMA LIEBOWITZ WAS A PROMINENT SCHOLAR AND EDUCATOR IN THE FIELD OF JEWISH BIBLICAL COMMENTARY. HER TEACHINGS AND INSIGHTS CONTINUE TO INFLUENCE GENERATIONS OF STUDENTS AND SCHOLARS AROUND THE WORLD.

Oh, how I am filled with thoughts and musings after reading Parashat Vayikra. This portion of the Torah has spoken to me in a way that has left me feeling both contemplative and inspired. The central theme of sacrifice and the offering of one's self for the sake of others is a concept that I find both beautiful and profound.

As I reflect upon the teachings of Vayikra, I am reminded of the words of Don Quixote, who once said, "Love and a cough cannot be hid." In the same way, the act of sacrifice, too, cannot be hidden. It is an outward expression of love and devotion to the divine, a demonstration of one's commitment to doing what is right, no matter the cost.

The offering of animals as sacrifices in the time of the Temple was not simply a physical act, but a symbol of the surrender of one's own will. It was a way of acknowledging that all that we have comes from the hand of God and must be returned in gratitude. This is a powerful message, one that reminds us to be mindful of the blessings we receive and to be generous in our offerings to others.

But sacrifice is not limited to the offering of physical possessions. In this age, we are called upon to offer something much more valuable – our hearts. We are asked to give of ourselves, to lay aside our own desires, to be kind and compassionate to those in need, and to love our neighbor as ourselves. This is the greatest sacrifice of all, and it is something that we can all strive to do, in our own way.

In conclusion, I am grateful for the teachings of Parashat Vayikra and the reminder that sacrifice and love are the foundation of a meaningful life. Let us continue to seek the divine by giving of ourselves, whether it be through our time, resources, or love. As Don Quixote said, "Virtue is not left to stand alone. He who practices it will have neighbors."

> *MIGUEL DE CERVANTES WAS A SPANISH WRITER AND AUTHOR OF THE FAMOUS NOVEL DON QUIXOTE, WHICH IS CONSIDERED ONE OF THE MOST INFLUENTIAL WORKS OF LITERATURE IN HISTORY. HE IS KNOWN FOR HIS CONTRIBUTIONS TO THE SPANISH GOLDEN AGE AND HIS INNOVATIVE USE OF LITERARY DEVICES SUCH AS METAFICTION AND SATIRE.*

TZAV

In the style of Rumi

Oh my soul, let us journey together, to the depths of Parashat Tzav. To the land of smoke and fire, where the offerings are burnt and the sacrifices are made.

Here in this place, the Kohanim, the priests, are called upon to serve, to tend to the altar, to perform the sacred rites. And yet, the real work of the priest is not in the offerings, but in the state of their hearts.

For the true offering is not the lamb, nor the grain, nor the incense. The true offering is the pure and humble heart, the heart that is ready to serve and to sacrifice, the heart that is open to the light of God.

And as we watch the smoke rise and the fire consume the offerings, let us turn our hearts to the fire within us, the fire that burns away the impurities, the fire that purifies and transforms.

Let us offer our hearts to the Divine, let us offer our love and our devotion, let us offer our pain and our joy. Let us burn away the old, and let the new be born, let the light of God shine within us, let the fire of love consume us.

And as we watch the smoke rise, let us be reminded of the transience of all things, the impermanence of life, the fleeting nature of existence. And let us turn our hearts to the eternal, to the unchanging, to the infinite.

For in the smoke, we see the mystery, the beauty, the wonder of existence. We see the unity of all things, the connectedness of all beings, the unity of the soul and the divine.

And as we return from this journey, let us carry the fire of love within us, let us be a light in the world, let us be a beacon of hope, let us be the priests of our own lives, the servants of the divine.

For in the offering of our hearts, in the sacrifice of our love, we find the ultimate fulfillment, the true purpose of our existence, the deep and abiding joy of the soul.

So let us journey together, oh my soul, to the depths of Parashat Tzav, and let the fire of love consume us, and let the light of God shine within us, now and forevermore. Amen.

Rumi was a 13th-century Persian poet, scholar, and Sufi mystic who has become one of the most widely read poets in the world. His poetry is known for its spiritual and philosophical themes, and has inspired millions of people across the globe.

Parashat Tzav is a portion of the Torah that deals with the rituals and duties of the priests, who served as intermediaries between the Israelites and God. This section highlights the importance of communal ritual in maintaining social cohesion and reinforcing the values and beliefs of a community. Let us explore the social functions of these rituals and their role in shaping the collective consciousness of the Israelites.

Society is a product of collective representations and that rituals serve as the embodiment of these representations. In Parashat Tzav, the rituals described are not simply religious acts, but also serve as a means of reinforcing the beliefs and values of the Israelites. For example, the daily offerings of the priests symbolize the importance of sacrifice and obedience to God, which are key values of the Israelite community. Similarly, the use of incense in the ritual symbolizes the purification and sanctification of the sanctuary, which reinforces the idea of God's presence and the importance of keeping the space holy.

Rituals also serve as a means of social integration, bringing individuals together and reinforcing the bonds between them. This is evident in Parashat Tzav, where the priests are described as working together to perform the offerings and maintain the sanctuary. The communal nature of the rituals underscores the idea that the community is united in its worship and devotion to God, which reinforces social cohesion and strengthens the bonds between its members.

Finally, rituals have a powerful emotional impact, evoking strong feelings of awe, reverence, and sanctity. In Parashat Tzav, the descriptions of the offerings and the rituals performed by the priests are imbued with a sense of majesty and reverence, emphasizing the importance of the sacred in the lives of the Israelites. The emotional impact of the rituals reinforces the values and beliefs of the community, shaping the collective consciousness and inspiring individuals to act in accordance with the norms and expectations of the group.

In conclusion, Parashat Tzav provides a clear illustration of the importance of communal ritual in reinforcing the values and beliefs of a community. Through its description of the duties and rituals of the priests, the Torah highlights the power of ritual to evoke strong emotions, reinforce social bonds, and shape the collective consciousness. Through the lens of sociology, it becomes clear that the communal rituals described in Parashat

Tzav serve a critical role in maintaining the social cohesion and cultural identity of the Israelite community.

> *Emile Durkheim was a French sociologist who is considered as one of the founding fathers of sociology. He is known for his contributions to the development of social theory, social research methods, and the study of suicide.*

Parashat Tzav is a fascinating portion of the Torah that speaks to the heart of Jewish ritual and tradition. I believe that the study of Jewish texts and traditions is a powerful way to deepen our connection to our heritage and to the sacred. In this essay, I will explore the themes and insights of Parashat Tzav through the lens of Jewish cultural anthropology and the meaning of Jewish tradition.

One of the key themes of Parashat Tzav is the idea of sacrifice and offerings. The portion details the various types of offerings that were made in the ancient Temple, including burnt offerings, grain offerings, and peace offerings. These offerings were seen as a way of connecting to God and expressing gratitude for God's blessings. Through the act of sacrifice, the people of Israel were able to express their commitment to their faith and to the relationship between God and their community.

I am particularly interested in the cultural and symbolic significance of Jewish rituals and traditions, including the idea of sacrifice. Rituals and traditions serve a crucial role in helping people to connect to their cultural and spiritual heritage, and to understand their place in the world. These rituals and traditions help to anchor us in our communities, and to provide a sense of meaning and purpose.

In Parashat Tzav, we can see this idea of sacrifice and offerings as a powerful form of communal expression. Through the act of sacrifice, the people of Israel were able to come together and express their shared values and beliefs. This helped to create a sense of community, and to strengthen the bonds between the people.

In addition to the theme of sacrifice, Parashat Tzav also speaks to the idea of ritual and tradition as a means of connecting to the divine. In this portion, we see the priests, the kohanim, being anointed and consecrated for their service in the Temple. This anointing was seen as a way of marking the priests as special, and of endowing them with the sacred power to perform their duties.

I believe that this idea of ritual and tradition as a means of connecting to the divine is at the heart of Jewish spirituality. Through the study of our traditions, we are able to deepen our connection to our heritage, to our ancestors, and to the sacred. Through the practice of ritual, we are able to connect to the transcendent, and to experience a sense of awe and reverence.

In conclusion, Parashat Tzav is a powerful and meaningful portion of the Torah that speaks to the heart of Jewish tradition and spirituality. Through its themes of sacrifice and offerings, and of ritual and tradition as a means of connecting to the divine, it teaches us about the importance of our cultural and spiritual heritage, and the role that traditions play in our lives. I believe that the study and practice of these traditions is a powerful way to deepen our connection to the sacred, and to understand our place in the world.

> *Barbara Myerhoff was an American anthropologist, folklorist, and filmmaker who focused on the study of Jewish culture and aging. She is best known for her award-winning documentary film "Number Our Days" and her book "Lifetimes: A Beautiful Way to Explain Death to Children."*

SHMINI

In the style of Aaron, the High Priest

Dear God,

I am writing to express my anger and disappointment over the deaths of my sons, Nadav and Avihu. I cannot understand why you would take them away from me in such a sudden and cruel manner. They were young, full of life, and had so much potential.

In Parashat Shemini, it was stated that they brought an "unauthorized fire" before you, and as a result, you consumed them with fire. However, I cannot help but feel that their punishment was unjust. They were following their instincts and desires, and did not intentionally cause harm. I cannot accept that they should be punished so severely for a mistake that was made out of reverence and love for you.

I am also disappointed in the fact that you did not give me a chance to mourn or grieve for my sons. Their deaths were sudden and abrupt, and I was not given the chance to say goodbye or honor their memory. The loss of my sons has been a heavy burden to bear, and I feel that you have abandoned me in my time of need.

God, I am angry and frustrated with you for taking my sons away from me. I do not understand why you would cause such pain and suffering to your faithful servants. I hope that in time, I can come to terms with their deaths, but for now, I am filled with anger and sadness.

Sincerely,

Aaron

> *Aaron was the older brother of Moses and the first High Priest of Israel.*

God: Aaron, my son, it is with a heavy heart that I come to you today to discuss the deaths of your sons, Nadav and Avihu.

Aaron: Lord, I am ready to hear what you have to say.

God: Aaron, you know that I am a God of holiness and that I require complete obedience from those who serve me. Your sons did not follow my commands and offered incense before me without being told to do so.

Aaron: Lord, I did not know of their intentions. They acted on their own accord.

God: That may be so, Aaron, but as the High Priest, you are responsible for the actions of those under your charge. I had to show my authority and holiness to the Israelites, and your sons' actions provided me with the opportunity to do so.

Aaron: I understand, Lord. I am heartbroken at the loss of my sons, but I accept your judgment.

God: Aaron, I do not take pleasure in taking lives, but it was necessary for the preservation of my holiness and to teach the Israelites about the importance of obedience. I promise that I will be with you and your family in this time of mourning.

Aaron: Thank you, Lord. I trust in your wisdom and mercy.

God: You have always been a faithful servant, Aaron. I will continue to bless you and your family. Be strong, for I am with you always.

In the Style of the Mother of Nadav and Avihu

Dear God,

I am writing this letter with a heavy heart and immense anger. I am the mother of Nadav and Avihu, two of your most devoted servants, who were taken from me far too soon.

Why, God? Why did you take my sons from me? They were good men, they lived their lives according to your laws and served you with all their hearts. And yet, you took them away without a second thought. I cannot understand why you would do this to me, to their families, to the community.

I am furious at you for your cruelty. You give us children and then take them away, leaving us to suffer and grieve for the rest of our lives. You are supposed to be a loving and compassionate God, but I cannot see that in your actions. You show no mercy to those who serve you, and it makes me question why anyone would ever choose to follow you.

I demand answers, God. Why did you take my sons from me? What was the reason behind their deaths? Was it a mistake? Was it punishment? I need to know, so I can have some semblance of peace and closure.

I am filled with rage, and it is directed at you. You have broken my heart and destroyed my family, and I will never forgive you for that. I cannot continue to worship a God who acts with such cruelty and disregard for human life.

Sincerely,

A Grieving Mother

> *The mother of Nadav and Avihu is not mentioned by name in the Bible. However, according to Jewish tradition, her name was Elisheva and she was the daughter of Amminadab and sister of Nachshon, both prominent leaders in the Israelite community.*

TAZRIA

In the style of Mary Seacole

Oh, my dear friends, what a week it has been since we last gathered here to reflect on the teachings of our Lord. This week, we read from the book of Leviticus, Parashat Tazria, which spoke of the laws of ritual impurity, especially as it pertains to childbirth and skin diseases.

As a nurse and healer, I must say that these laws touched a chord in my heart. For many years, I have travelled the world, tending to the sick and injured, and I have seen firsthand how easily disease can spread, especially in places where hygiene is poor and people live in close quarters.

For you see, dear friends, cleanliness is of utmost importance in the healing arts. It is what keeps both the patient and the healer safe from harm. And in this context, the Lord's laws on ritual impurity, especially after childbirth, serve as a reminder that we must always be mindful of the health and well-being of those in our care.

And yet, I must also confess that I have seen how these laws have been used to discriminate against certain groups of people, particularly those who are deemed to be unclean due to their race or their social status. And this breaks my heart, for it goes against the very essence of what it means to be a nurse and a healer.

For I believe that all human beings are worthy of compassion and care, regardless of their background or station in life. And so, I call upon all of us to remember the Lord's teachings in Parashat Tazria, but to also put them into practice with love and kindness in our hearts. For it is only then that we will truly be fulfilling our roles as servants of the Lord and healers of God's people.

> *Mary Seacole was a Jamaican-born nurse and businesswoman who gained recognition for her work in caring for wounded British soldiers during the Crimean War. Despite facing racial and gender discrimination, she was known for her bravery, compassion, and dedication to improving the lives of others.*

Parashat Tazria, one of the weekly readings from the Torah, details the laws of ritual purity and impurity related to skin diseases and childbirth. The concepts of purity and impurity can be understood in terms of the physical and spiritual well-being of the individual.

The laws of ritual purity and impurity serve to promote health and prevent disease. The physical aspects of these laws, such as the requirement for isolation of individuals with skin diseases, serve to prevent the spread of infectious diseases and protect the health of the community. Similarly, the laws related to childbirth are designed to ensure the well-being of both the mother and the child, promoting both physical and spiritual health.

The connection between ritual purity and medicine can also be seen in the role of the physician. In my "Guide for the Perplexed," I write that the physician must be guided by both scientific knowledge and moral virtue. The physician must not only have a deep understanding of the human body and the causes of disease, but must also be guided by principles of justice, compassion, and respect for the dignity of the patient.

In this light, the laws of ritual purity in Parashat Tazria can be seen as an expression of the moral and ethical values that should guide the practice of medicine. The physician must be concerned not only with the physical health of the patient, but also with their spiritual well-being and the preservation of their dignity.

Thus, the laws of ritual purity and impurity in Parashat Tazria serve as a reminder of the interconnectedness of physical and spiritual health, and of the importance of both scientific knowledge and moral virtue in the practice of medicine. By promoting health and preventing disease, these laws help to ensure the well-being of the individual and the community, fulfilling the divine purpose of healing and restoration.

Moses Maimonides was a Jewish philosopher, theologian, and physician who lived in the 12th century. He is considered one of the most influential figures in Jewish intellectual history and is best known for his works on Jewish law and philosophy, including the Mishneh Torah and the Guide for the Perplexed.

As a scientist and physician, Parashat Tazria holds a special significance for me, as it highlights the importance of healing and the role of the community in promoting health and wellness. The Torah teaches that when an individual contracts a skin disease, they must be isolated from the community until they have been declared pure by the priests. This symbolizes the community's responsibility to protect itself from illness, and to support those who are sick in their journey to wellness.

Similarly, in my work as a virologist, I saw firsthand the power of community in fighting disease. With the development of the polio vaccine, I was able to harness the collective efforts of millions of people to eradicate a devastating illness. The vaccine was not simply a product of my own work, but a collective effort of thousands of individuals, each doing their part to promote health and wellness.

Parashat Tazria also reminds us of the importance of humility and compassion in our interactions with those who are sick. The Torah emphasizes that those with skin diseases must be treated with dignity and respect, even as they are separated from the community. Similarly, in my work, I saw that effective healing requires a deep understanding of the human experience and the capacity to empathize with those who are suffering.

In conclusion, Parashat Tazria and my work as a physician and scientist are inextricably linked. Both emphasize the importance of community, compassion, and humility in promoting health and wellness. I am grateful for the lessons that the Torah has taught me, and for the opportunity to contribute to the well-being of humanity through my work.

> *Jonas Salk was an American virologist who developed the first successful polio vaccine, which has saved millions of lives worldwide. He dedicated his life to medical research and left a lasting legacy in the field of public health.*

METZORA

As a self-reflexive language, ritual has always been a central aspect of religious practice. In Parashat Metzora, the ritual of purification for a person affected by a skin disease is described in detail. The ritual involves a series of actions, such as the shaving of hair, washing of clothes and the application of certain oils and ashes to the affected area.

One can reflect on the significance of such rituals in shaping the collective consciousness and the individual's relationship to their faith. Rituals are a form of expression that carry the collective memory of a people, transmitting their values and beliefs from one generation to the next. The act of repeating these rituals reinforces the cultural and historical context of a particular people and gives meaning to their existence.

In the case of Parashat Metzora, the ritual of purification serves to remind the individual of the importance of spiritual purity and the need to maintain a harmonious relationship with God and with the community. The act of purification is not simply a physical process, but a spiritual one as well, as the person must confess their sins and make amends for their actions. This process of purification helps to foster a sense of self-awareness and accountability in the individual, leading them to a greater understanding of their own relationship to God and to their fellow human beings.

Furthermore, the use of oils and ashes in the purification process can be seen as a symbol of renewal and transformation. The ashes represent the purification of the past, the shedding of old ways of being, and the embracing of a new way of living. The oils, on the other hand, symbolize the nourishment and revitalization of the body, representing the renewal of life and the potential for growth and transformation.

In conclusion, the ritual of purification in Parashat Metzora is a powerful expression of the religious values and beliefs of the Jewish people. Through its repeated performance, it reinforces the collective memory and provides a means for individuals to connect with their faith and to develop a deeper understanding of their relationship to God and to their community. Rituals are a unique form of expression that shape the collective consciousness and provide a means for transmitting cultural and historical meaning from one generation to the next.

WALTER BENJAMIN WAS A GERMAN PHILOSOPHER, CULTURAL CRITIC AND ESSAYIST. HE IS BEST KNOWN FOR HIS WORK ON THE CONCEPT OF AURA IN ART AND FOR HIS ANALYSIS OF MODERNITY AND CAPITALISM.

In the style of Betty Friedan

As a woman and a scholar, I have always been intrigued by the intersections of gender, religion, and culture. This week's Parashat Metzora, with its focus on impurities and physical afflictions, has given me a chance to reflect on the role of gender in our understanding of these concepts.

The limitations and restrictions placed on women in society lead to a sense of dissatisfaction and unhappiness. I see the portrayal of impurities in Parashat Metzora as a reflection of patriarchal attitudes towards women and their bodies.

The physical afflictions described in the parasha, such as skin diseases, leprosy, and bodily discharges, are often seen as punishments for sin or immoral behavior. These diseases were seen as a mark of shame, and those who suffered from them were ostracized and excluded from society. This notion of impurity is inherently gendered, as it is only women who are considered to be impure during menstruation, and this impurity is seen as a negative thing.

This understanding of impurities as a reflection of sin and moral failing, as well as the gendered nature of these impurities, reinforces patriarchal attitudes towards women and their bodies. It perpetuates the idea that women's bodies are inherently flawed and in need of control and regulation. This notion of impurity also reinforces the idea that women are responsible for maintaining the purity of society and the community.

As we read Parashat Metzora, it is important to reflect on the role of gender in our understanding of impurities and physical afflictions. We must question the ways in which patriarchal attitudes have influenced our interpretation of these concepts, and work towards a more inclusive and empowering understanding of these issues.

In conclusion, Parashat Metzora provides an opportunity to reflect on the intersections of gender, religion, and culture, and to question the ways in which patriarchal attitudes have shaped our understanding of these concepts. We must continue to challenge these attitudes and work towards a more inclusive and empowering understanding of these issues.

Betty Friedan was an American feminist, social activist, and writer who fought for the equality of women through her influential book "The Feminine Mystique."

In the style of Franz Boas

As I reflect on Parashat Metzora, I am struck by the connection between the leprosy described in this portion of the Torah and the anthropological concepts of taboo and purity.

The study of culture is essential to understanding the human experience. The way people think, feel and behave is shaped by the cultural norms and values that they learn from childhood. In Parashat Metzora, we see how the laws of leprosy and ritual purity were used to regulate and control the behavior of the Israelites.

The laws of leprosy in this portion of the Torah are examples of the cultural taboo. Taboos are cultural norms that regulate behavior by prohibiting or restricting certain activities or objects. The laws of leprosy in Parashat Metzora regulated the behavior of the Israelites by prohibiting them from engaging in certain activities or touching certain objects if they were infected with the disease. This was a way of ensuring that the community remained pure and protected from disease.

Cultural norms and values are related to the concept of purity. People are often motivated by the desire to maintain purity and avoid contamination. In Parashat Metzora, we see how the laws of leprosy and ritual purity were used to maintain the purity of the Israelites. The laws regulated their behavior, including their interactions with others, to ensure that the community remained pure.

In conclusion, Parashat Metzora provides valuable insights into the cultural norms and values of the Israelites. Through the connection between the laws of leprosy and the anthropological concepts of taboo and purity, we can understand how cultural norms and values shaped the behavior of the Israelites and helped to regulate and protect their community. This serves as a reminder of the important role that culture plays in shaping human experience and behavior.

Franz Boas was a German-American anthropologist and cultural relativist who greatly impacted the field of cultural anthropology and shaped our understanding of human diversity.

ACHAREI MOT

In my song "You Want It Darker," I explore echoes of similar themes that can be found in the biblical portion Acharei Mot.

The lyrics, "Hineni, hineni, I'm ready, my Lord," reference the response of Abraham in the book of Genesis when God calls upon him to sacrifice his son Isaac. This expression of submission to a higher power is echoed in the portion of Acharei Mot, where the Israelites are called upon to make atonement for their sins through sacrifice.

Our relationship with the divine is a complex and often difficult one. "If you are the dealer, I'm out of the game," point to a sense of disillusionment with religious authority. This idea is reflected in the portion of Acharei Mot, where the Israelites are warned against misusing their relationship with God for personal gain.

Furthermore, our connection with the divine is a constant struggle, requiring us to continually seek atonement and redemption. "If you want it darker, we kill the flame." Darkness and death are necessary for renewal and rebirth. Similarly, the portion of Acharei Mot emphasizes the importance of continually seeking atonement and purification.

Our relationship with the divine is a complex and challenging one, requiring us to constantly seek redemption and renewal. Through this struggle, however, we can find a deeper sense of meaning and purpose in life.

LEONARD COHEN WAS A CANADIAN SINGER-SONGWRITER, POET, AND NOVELIST. HE WAS KNOWN FOR HIS DEEP, RICH VOICE AND HIS INTROSPECTIVE AND INSIGHTFUL LYRICS.

As a writer, I often find solace in the words and stories of the Torah, and this week's parashah, Acharei Mot, is no exception. The story of the death of Aaron's two sons, Nadav and Avihu, is a tragedy that resonates deeply with me, as it does with many of us who have experienced loss.

But what I admire about this parashat is the wisdom it imparts about the experience of tragedy and how to endure it. The story tells us that Nadav and Avihu brought "strange fire" into the Tabernacle, and they were consumed by a fire from God. Despite the shock and sadness of Aaron and the people, God commanded Moses to instruct Aaron and his surviving sons to endure and carry on their duties as priests.

This story speaks to the resilience and fortitude that is required of us when we face tragedy. It is a reminder that even in the midst of loss, we must continue to live our lives and fulfill our responsibilities. The wisdom to endure is a powerful one, and it is something that I have come to understand more fully through my own experiences.

As a woman living in the 17th century, I have faced much tragedy in my own life. I lost my husband, children, and other loved ones, and yet I have continued to write, to reflect on my experiences, and to share my wisdom with others. Just as Aaron was commanded to endure and continue his duties, I too have found that my own duties and responsibilities have given me a sense of purpose and meaning during difficult times.

The wisdom of the Torah is that we must not give up in the face of tragedy, but instead we must find the strength to endure and to carry on. Whether it is through our work, our relationships, or our spiritual practice, we must find ways to channel our grief and continue to live our lives.

In conclusion, the story of Acharei Mot teaches us about the experience of tragedy and the wisdom to endure. It reminds us that even in the face of loss, we must continue to live our lives and fulfill our responsibilities. This is a powerful message that has sustained me through my own struggles, and I believe it will be a source of comfort and inspiration for generations to come.

GLÜCKEL OF HAMELN WAS A JEWISH BUSINESSWOMAN AND WRITER BORN IN 1646 IN HAMBURG, GERMANY. SHE IS KNOWN FOR HER MEMOIRS, WHICH PROVIDE A DETAILED ACCOUNT OF HER LIFE AND THE JEWISH COMMUNITY IN 17TH CENTURY GERMANY.

In the style of Franz Kafka

In parashat Acharei Mot, there is a scene that takes place in the holy of holies, where only the high priest is allowed to enter once a year on Yom Kippur. This serves as a setting for the idea of access to the holy, as it highlights the restrictions and limitations placed on those seeking entry.

This raises questions of power and authority and the ways in which individuals are oppressed by these forces. Acharei Mot can be seen as a manifestation of these themes, as the high priest must navigate the restrictions placed upon him in order to access the holy.

As the high priest enters the holy of holies, he must first remove his outer garment and adorn himself with the sacred vestments, symbolizing his detachment from the secular world and his purity. He then approaches the holy, offering incense and atoning for the sins of the people, making him the mediator between the people and God.

However, this trial is not without its difficulties. The high priest must be without blemish, both physically and morally, and he must take great care in his actions, for one mistake could cost him his life. This demonstrates the strictness of the restrictions placed upon him, and the consequences that come with violating them.

This rituals of access to the holy highlight the unequal distribution of power and authority in the world. The high priest is privileged to access the holy, but he must first pass through a series of restrictions and limitations. Meanwhile, the people are excluded from the holy and must rely on the high priest as their mediator.

Furthermore, the high priest's role as mediator raises questions about the nature of access to the holy. Does the high priest have a special connection with God, or is his role merely symbolic? Is access to the holy limited to the high priest, or is it accessible to all people? These questions demonstrate the complex nature of access to the holy and the ways in which power and authority shape our understanding of it.

> *Franz Kafka was a German-speaking Bohemian novelist and short-story writer, widely regarded as one of the major figures of 20th-century literature. His work, which explores themes of alienation, anxiety, and absurdity, has had a significant impact on modern literature and popular culture.*

KEDOSHIM

IN THE STYLE OF BETTY BERZON

In Parashat Kedoshim, we find a significant portion of the Torah dedicated to laws that promote holiness and ethical behavior. In this portion, we encounter various commandments related to sexual ethics, including the prohibition of homosexuality, bestiality, and incest.

However, it's important to note that the commandments in Parashat Kedoshim were written in the context of ancient Israelite society and are reflective of the cultural values of that time. In contemporary times, our understanding of sexuality and relationships has changed, and many people who identify as gay, lesbian, bisexual, or transgender may find these commandments challenging and hurtful.

In my book "Permanent Partners: Building Gay & Lesbian Relationships That Last," I write about the importance of understanding the changing attitudes towards sexuality and relationships. Modern society has come a long way in recognizing the legitimacy of same-sex relationships, and this shift has been driven by a growing awareness of the complexities of human sexuality.

The Torah's commandments regarding sexuality should not be viewed as absolute and unchanging, but rather as an expression of the cultural values of ancient Israelite society. We should approach these commandments with an open mind and consider the context in which they were written.

Moreover, the primary goal of the Torah is to promote ethical behavior and encourage people to live lives that are meaningful and fulfilling. In this context, the commandments regarding sexuality should not be used to discriminate against people who identify as LGBT, but rather as a way to encourage people to live lives that are based on mutual respect and love.

In conclusion, the primary goal of the Torah is to promote ethical behavior and we should approach its commandments with an open mind and consider their contemporary relevance. In this way, we can ensure that the Torah continues to serve as a source of inspiration and guidance for all people, regardless of their sexual orientation or identity.

> *BETTY BERZON WAS A PIONEERING PSYCHOTHERAPIST AND AUTHOR WHO FOCUSED ON LGBTQ ISSUES AND RELATIONSHIPS. HER GROUNDBREAKING WORK HELPED TO SHIFT SOCIETAL ATTITUDES AND IMPROVE THE LIVES OF MANY IN THE LGBTQ COMMUNITY.*

IN THE STYLE OF RUDOLPH OTTO

In this week's parashah, Kedoshim, we are presented with the concept of holiness and its significance in the Jewish faith. This idea of holiness is not unique to Judaism, as similar concepts can be found in other religions, such as Islam and Christianity.

The holiness described in Kedoshim is characterized by a separation from the mundane and a devotion to the divine. This is the "numinous," an overwhelming sense of the sacred that elicits feelings of awe and reverence. Just as the numinous evokes a sense of the transcendent, the holiness described in Kedoshim calls upon the Jewish people to set themselves apart and dedicate themselves to a higher purpose.

However, while the concept of holiness may be universal, its expression and manifestation differ between religions. In Kedoshim, holiness is achieved through adherence to the commandments and laws given by God, while in other religions it may be attained through spiritual practices or devotion to a particular deity.

Furthermore, the emphasis placed on holiness also varies between religions. In some traditions, holiness is seen as an end in and of itself, while in others it is viewed as a means to an ultimate goal, such as union with the divine or liberation from the cycle of rebirth.

Despite these differences, the common thread running through all expressions of holiness is the idea that there is a higher reality that transcends our everyday experiences. This recognition of the sacred and the transcendent is a powerful reminder of the infinite possibilities that exist beyond our limited understanding and the importance of dedicating ourselves to a higher purpose.

In conclusion, the concept of holiness in Kedoshim serves as a powerful reminder of the significance of the divine in our lives and the importance of setting ourselves apart in devotion to a higher purpose. This idea of holiness, while expressed differently in various religions, serves as a testament to the universal recognition of the sacred and the transcendent.

RUDOLF OTTO WAS A GERMAN LUTHERAN THEOLOGIAN AND PHILOSOPHER WHO IS BEST KNOWN FOR HIS GROUNDBREAKING WORK, "THE IDEA OF THE HOLY." HE WAS ALSO A KEY FIGURE IN THE DEVELOPMENT OF THE STUDY OF COMPARATIVE RELIGION.

The concepts of sexual morality and ethics is central to the teachings of Parashat Kedoshim. The Torah commands that sexual activity should be limited to heterosexual relationships between a man and a woman who are married to each other, but I view sexual orientation as a complex and multi-dimensional aspect of a person's identity. Individuals can have multiple and varying degrees of attraction to different gender groups and these attractions can change over time. Sexual orientation is not a choice, but rather an innate aspect of an individual's identity that cannot be altered or changed.

My views on sexuality align with the teachings of Parashat Kedoshim in that both emphasize the importance of ethical and respectful sexual behavior. In the Torah, it is stated that one should not engage in sexual relations with someone who is not one's spouse. This commandment is intended to preserve the sanctity of marriage and to ensure that sexual activity is respectful and responsible.

Similarly, I believe that sexual behavior should be grounded in consent, respect, and mutual enjoyment. Individuals should be free to express their sexuality in ways that are consistent with their personal values and beliefs. However, sexual activity should never be used as a means of exploitation or abuse.

In conclusion, the Torah believes that sexual activity should be limited to heterosexual relationships between a married man and woman, while I believe that sexual orientation is an innate aspect of an individual's identity that should be expressed in ways that are respectful and consensual. Both the Torah and my views emphasize the need for individuals to approach sexual behavior with reverence, respect, and responsibility.

Fritz Klein was a German-American psychiatrist and psychoanalyst, known for his groundbreaking work in the field of sexual orientation and gender identity. He is particularly remembered for his creation of the Klein Sexual Orientation Grid, a tool for assessing sexual orientation.

EMOR

In the style of Yosef Yerushalmi

In Parashat Emor, time and memory play a significant role in the religious and cultural practices of the Jewish people. Through the commandments and rituals outlined in this portion of the Torah, the Jewish community is able to connect with their ancestral heritage and maintain a sense of continuity with their past.

One of the central themes in Emor is the concept of time and the cyclical nature of the Jewish calendar. The section describes the various holidays and their respective dates, including Passover, Shavuot, Rosh Hashanah, Yom Kippur, Sukkot, and Shemini Atzeret. Each holiday serves as a marker in the Jewish calendar and is a reminder of the significant events in Jewish history.

For example, Passover commemorates the Israelites' liberation from slavery in Egypt and their journey to the Promised Land. Shavuot marks the giving of the Torah at Mount Sinai. Rosh Hashanah and Yom Kippur are days of repentance and reflection, while Sukkot celebrates the harvest and the temporary shelters used by the Israelites during their journey in the wilderness. Through these holidays, the Jewish people are able to connect with their history and the events that shaped their identity as a people.

In addition to marking important moments in history, the holidays also serve as opportunities for the Jewish community to connect with their ancestors. Through the repeated performance of these rituals, the Jewish people are able to maintain a sense of continuity with their past and preserve their ancestral heritage.

The idea of memory is also emphasized in Emor through the concept of the sabbatical year. Every seven years, the land was to be allowed to rest and all debts were to be forgiven. This was seen as a way of remembering the struggles of their ancestors and the importance of humility and compassion. The sabbatical year served as a reminder of the struggles of the past and the importance of treating each other with compassion and mercy.

In conclusion, Parashat Emor highlights the significance of time and memory in the religious and cultural practices of the Jewish people. Through the commandments and rituals outlined in this portion of the Torah, the Jewish community is able to connect with their ancestral heritage and maintain a sense of continuity with their past. These practices serve as reminders of the important events in Jewish history and the struggles of their ancestors, and provide opportunities for the Jewish people to connect with their past and preserve their cultural heritage.

Yosef Yerushalmi was an Israeli-American historian and professor of Jewish history at Columbia University. He was known for his scholarly works on the history of Jewish culture and religion.

The idea of time travel has always fascinated me, and as the Doctor, I have witnessed many incredible events and celebrations throughout the universe. In a way, time travel is similar to these holidays. It allows us to explore different times and places, to witness history unfold, and to connect with our past. Just like the Jewish holidays, time travel provides us with a glimpse into different cultures and ways of life, and it allows us to appreciate the diversity of humanity.

Parashat Emor, with its laws and commandments, represents a timeless tradition that has been passed down from generation to generation. The Jewish holidays, with their rich history and customs, provide a sense of continuity and stability in an ever-changing universe. In many ways, they are a celebration of time itself, marking the passage of the years and the cycles of nature.

But as I travel through time, I also realize the fragility of these celebrations. The forces of darkness and evil seek to disrupt and destroy the traditions that bring light and hope to the universe. It is up to us to protect these sacred celebrations, to ensure that they endure for generations to come.

In my travels, I have seen how different cultures and civilizations have their own celebrations and traditions, each unique and special in its own way. And yet, despite the vast differences between them, there is a common thread that runs through them all: the celebration of life and the passage of time.

In this spirit, I encourage all those who read this to embrace the traditions of Parashat Emor and the Jewish holidays, to celebrate their heritage and to pass on the lessons and stories of their ancestors to future generations.

As the Doctor, I have seen the power of time and tradition to bring people together, to heal wounds and to create a brighter future.

So, my dear friends, whether you are a Time Lord like myself, or simply a human observing these holidays, I encourage you to take a moment to reflect on the significance of Parashat Emor, the Jewish holidays, and the concept of time travel. Let us cherish our history, celebrate our traditions, and embrace the diversity of life.

And with that, I bid you farewell. Exterminate! Er, I mean, farewell. The Doctor, over and out.

The Doctor is a Time Lord from the planet Gallifrey who travels through time and space in the TARDIS, fighting evil and helping those in need. With his quick wit and boundless curiosity, he is one of the greatest heroes in the universe.

Parashat Emor is part of the Book of Leviticus, a volume that that outlines the laws, regulations, and rituals of the Jewish community. As a scholar of religion, I find these texts to be a fascinating examination of the social structures, values, and beliefs of ancient Judaism.

All religious systems are based on the principle of "purity," which is a moral concept that defines what is acceptable and unacceptable in society. The laws and rituals of a religious community reflect its underlying values and beliefs, and that these laws and rituals serve to maintain the moral order of society.

In this light, Parashat Emor and Leviticus can be seen as a reflection of the moral and social order of ancient Judaism. Through its laws and regulations, the text outlines what is considered pure and impure in the Jewish community, and provides guidance on how to maintain the moral order through rituals and practices. For example, the laws on kosher food, the restrictions on sexual relations, and the commandments to observe the Sabbath all serve to define the boundaries of acceptable behavior and to maintain the purity of the Jewish community.

Additionally, ritual is not simply a symbolic representation of a belief, but is a social and cultural act that helps to reinforce the values and beliefs of a community. In Parashat Emor, this can be seen in the many rituals and ceremonies described, including the celebration of the Sabbath, the Passover sacrifice, and the Day of Atonement. These rituals serve to reinforce the moral and social order of the Jewish community and to connect the individual to the wider community and its shared values and beliefs.

Finally, religious systems are not static but are constantly evolving and adapting to new cultural and social pressures. This can be seen in the history of Jewish law, which developed and changed over time to reflect the changing needs and values of the Jewish community. In this light, Parashat Emor can be seen as a snapshot of the moral and social order of ancient Judaism, and a testament to the dynamic nature of religious systems.

In conclusion, the study of Parashat Emor provides insight into the moral, social, and cultural values of ancient Judaism. Through its laws, rituals, and ceremonies, the text reflects the underlying beliefs and values of the Jewish community and serves to maintain the moral order of society. By exploring the themes and ideas present in Parashat Emor, we can gain a deeper understanding of the complexities of religious systems and the role they play in shaping the social and cultural landscape.

> *MARY DOUGLAS (1921-2007) WAS A PROMINENT BRITISH ANTHROPOLOGIST, KNOWN FOR HER CONTRIBUTIONS TO CULTURAL THEORY AND SOCIAL ANTHROPOLOGY. HER WORK FOCUSED ON THE WAYS IN WHICH CULTURE AND SOCIAL ORGANIZATION SHAPE HUMAN BEHAVIOR AND THOUGHT.*

BEHAR

In the Style of the Lorax

I speak for the earth, for what it doth say,
In Parashat Behar, a lesson we pray,
To cherish and care for this world so fair,
And harvest its gifts with love and with care.

The land, it is holy, a treasure divine,
It needs to be tended, its beauty to shine,
Sowing and reaping, but taking with care,
For we are its guardians, its servants aware.

The earth, it shall rest, for a season each year,
And we, in its honor, must make it all clear,
That we shall not take from its bounty so bright,
But cherish its gifts, in its beauty delight.

So listen, my friends, to the voice of the earth,
And guard it with care, with each moment, each mirth,
For we are its keepers, its guardians of grace,
And in Parashat Behar, its beauty we trace.

The Lorax is a furry, orange creature with a mustache who speaks for the trees and the environment. He is the titular character in Dr. Seuss' 1971 children's book, "The Lorax."

In the style of Shlomo Zemach

Parshat Behar is one of the most intriguing portions of the Torah, as it delves into the intricacies of agriculture and land ownership. This parsha is not only relevant for its religious significance, but also for its practical applications in the modern world, particularly in the realm of sustainable agriculture.

The principles outlined in Parshat Behar are crucial for a thriving agricultural system. They emphasize the importance of land rest, which is a crucial component of sustainable agriculture. According to the Torah, every seventh year, the land must be allowed to rest and recover, a concept known as shmita. This rest period provides an opportunity for the land to recover its fertility and rejuvenate, so that it can continue to produce crops for the next six years.

The principles of shmita also extend to the treatment of the land itself. The Torah mandates that the land must be treated with care and respect, with no overuse or abuse. This is a clear reference to the need for sustainable agriculture practices, where farmers must ensure that their land remains productive and healthy for future generations.

The Torah's teachings on agriculture offer a model for economic justice and equality. For example, the Torah mandates that the poor must be given access to land so that they can grow crops and feed their families. This is a powerful example of economic justice, as it ensures that everyone has access to the resources they need to survive and thrive.

Behar has a lot to offer the modern world in terms of sustainable agriculture and economic justice. The principles outlined in the parsha highlight the importance of land rest, the need for sustainable agriculture practices, and the value of economic equality. By following these principles, we can ensure that our agricultural systems are healthy, productive, and sustainable for generations to come.

> *Shlomo Zemach, an accomplished Israeli author, was a prominent figure in the field of agriculture and an influential pioneer of Zionism in the early 20th century. His contributions to the growth of Israeli agriculture and his writings on the subject have left a lasting impact on the country's development.*

IN THE STYLE OF JOHN MUIR

Parashat Behar, a section of the Torah that deals with the laws of the land and the concept of the sabbatical year, is a timeless lesson in the importance of preserving and respecting the earth. The sabbatical year, in which the land is to be left fallow and allowed to rejuvenate, is a concept that points to the delicate balance between man and nature and the need to respect and protect the land for future generations.

The land is not a resource to be exploited but a temple to be revered. The majesty of the land is a reflection of the divine, a place where God's handiwork was on display for all to see. The land is a sanctuary, a place of peace and solitude, where one can escape the stresses of modern life and be rejuvenated.

Parashat Behar speaks to this same idea, reminding us that the land is not just a commodity to be used for our own purposes but a gift from God, one that must be respected and preserved. The sabbatical year is a symbol of the importance of balance and renewal. By allowing the land to rest and rejuvenate, we ensure that it will be productive and healthy for future generations. This idea of preservation and conservation is echoed in Parashat Behar.

The land is a precious resource, one that is quickly being depleted by the forces of industrialization and development. We must fight to protect the wilderness areas where the land can be preserved for future generations.

Parashat Behar speaks to the same idea, reminding us that the land is a gift from God and one that must be respected and protected. The sabbatical year is a symbol of this idea, a reminder that we must take care of the land if we want it to continue to provide for us. By leaving the land fallow for a year, we ensure that it will be healthy and productive for generations to come.

In conclusion, Parashat Behar reminds us of the importance of respecting and preserving the land. Whether it is through the sabbatical year or the creation of national parks, the idea of preservation and conservation is a timeless lesson that speaks to the need to protect the earth for future generations. The land is a gift from God, a temple to be revered, and a place of peace and solitude. We must respect and protect it if we want it to continue to provide for us.

JOHN MUIR WAS A NATURALIST AND CONSERVATIONIST WHO IS OFTEN REFERRED TO AS THE "FATHER OF THE NATIONAL PARKS". HE WAS A KEY FIGURE IN THE ESTABLISHMENT OF YOSEMITE NATIONAL PARK AND FOUNDED THE SIERRA CLUB.

BECHUKOTAI

IN THE STYLE OF ROBERT COVER

In Parashat Bechukotai, we see God laying out the laws and regulations for the Israelites to follow. These laws cover various aspects of life, including agriculture, social interaction, and religious practices. One of the key themes in this Parashah is the idea that following these laws will bring blessings, while disobedience will result in curses.

For Robert Cover, a renowned legal scholar, law is much more than just a set of rules to be followed. He saw the law as a system of meaning that shapes and defines the society in which it operates. In his view, law is not just a means of regulating behavior but also a way of expressing and reinforcing social norms and values.

The laws outlined in Parashat Bechukotai, therefore, serve a much broader purpose than just regulating the behavior of the Israelites. They are also a way of expressing God's values and expectations for his people. By following these laws, the Israelites are not only obeying God's commandments but also contributing to the creation of a just and harmonious society.

Cover's perspective on the law highlights the importance of understanding the underlying values and principles that guide legal systems. It is not enough to simply follow the rules; we must also understand the broader societal goals that these rules serve. Only then can we truly appreciate the significance of legal systems and their role in shaping our world.

In conclusion, Parashat Bechukotai reminds us of the importance of law as a tool for shaping society and promoting justice. The laws outlined in this Parashah are not just a set of rules to be followed but also a reflection of God's values and expectations for his people. Understanding the deeper meaning and purpose of the law can help us appreciate its role in creating a just and equitable society.

ROBERT COVER (1943-1986) WAS AN INFLUENTIAL LEGAL SCHOLAR KNOWN FOR HIS WORK ON LEGAL THEORY, NARRATIVE, AND THE RELATIONSHIP BETWEEN LAW AND SOCIETY. HE TAUGHT AT YALE LAW SCHOOL FOR OVER A DECADE, LEAVING BEHIND A LASTING LEGACY IN THE FIELD OF LAW AND LITERATURE.

In the style of President Abraham Lincoln

As I reflect on Parashat Bechukotai, I am reminded of the obligations of citizenship and the importance of caring for one another. In this passage, God lays out the blessings and curses that will come to the people of Israel if they follow or depart from God's commands.

As I ponder these teachings, I cannot help but think of the struggles and challenges facing our own nation today. There are times when it seems as if division and hatred are winning the day, but I have faith that the good and noble qualities of the American people will ultimately triumph.

Just as the people of Israel were called upon to follow God's commandments, we as citizens have a responsibility to care for each other and work together for the betterment of our country. It is our obligation to help those in need, to be there for our neighbors, and to work for the common good.

As I have often said, "A house divided against itself cannot stand." We must come together, put aside our differences, and work towards a brighter future for all. Just as God promised the people of Israel to be with them, so too does God promise to be with us in our struggles and challenges.

Let us take heart from this promise, and strive to be worthy of the blessings that come from following God's commands. Let us work tirelessly to heal the wounds of division, to care for one another, and to build a stronger, more united nation. In doing so, we will honor the obligations of citizenship, and demonstrate the true spirit of compassion and generosity that are at the heart of our country's greatest ideals.

> *Abraham Lincoln was the 16th President of the United States, serving from 1861 until his assassination in 1865. He is widely considered one of America's greatest and most influential leaders, credited with preserving the Union during the Civil War and ending slavery through the Emancipation Proclamation.*

In the Style of Eve

As I sit here in the Garden of Eden, surrounded by the beauty and abundance of creation, I can't help but reflect on the words of Parashat Bechukotai and the authority of God. I know that I was created in the image of God, with a free will to choose my own path. Yet, as I hear the warning of punishments for disobedience, I feel frustrated with this understanding of God's authority.

Why must we always be threatened with punishment for our choices? Why can't we simply be trusted to make the right decisions and live in harmony with God and creation? Why must there always be a power dynamic in our relationship with God, with us constantly living in fear of losing favor and facing retribution?

I know that God is merciful and compassionate, but I struggle with this understanding of God's authority. I wish that we could have a deeper connection with God, one based on mutual love and respect rather than fear and obligation. I long for a relationship where we can be truly free to explore our own individuality, yet still be guided by the wisdom of God.

In a world where we are constantly told what to do and how to behave, I find myself searching for a more meaningful understanding of God's authority. I want to believe that God is not just a ruler, but a loving companion who is always there to support and guide us. I hope that one day, we can break free from the fear of punishment and find a more fulfilling connection with God.

Eve was the first woman.

NUMBERS/BEMIDBAR

The Book of Numbers and Rebellion

IN THE STYLE OF RABBI MENACHEM CREDITOR

The book of Numbers is a challenging and complex text that speaks to our time in many ways. As I've written elsewhere, "It is a story of the people of Israel wandering through the wilderness, struggling to find their way, and rebelling against the leadership of Moses and Aaron. It is a story of the human condition, of our tendency to rebel against authority and to question our place in the world."

This theme of rebellion is particularly relevant to our time, as we witness a new wave of social and political movements challenging traditional power structures and questioning the status quo. In many ways, these movements are fueled by new technologies that allow people to connect and organize in ways that were previously impossible.

The art of midrash, which is the Jewish tradition of interpreting and commenting on biblical texts, can help us to understand the relevance of the book of Numbers to our contemporary world. Midrash is a creative and imaginative process that allows us to engage with the text in new and meaningful ways, and to explore its themes and ideas in the context of our own lives.

One example of midrashic interpretation of the book of Numbers is the story of the rebellion of Korach, which is one of the most famous and dramatic episodes in the book. According to the biblical account, Korach led a rebellion against Moses and Aaron, arguing that they were taking too much power and authority for themselves. In response, Moses challenged Korach and his followers to a test, in which they would each offer incense before God, and the one who was accepted would be considered the true leader.

In midrashic interpretation, this story is seen as a cautionary tale about the dangers of rebellion and the importance of respecting authority. However, it can also be read as a call to question the legitimacy of authority and to challenge power structures that are unjust or oppressive. This is particularly relevant in our contemporary world, where new technologies are allowing people to organize and mobilize in ways that were previously impossible, and where traditional power structures are being challenged and transformed.

Overall, the book of Numbers and its themes of rebellion and wandering offer us a rich and complex text to explore and interpret through the art of midrash. By engaging with this text in creative and imaginative ways, we can deepen our understanding of its relevance to our contemporary world, and find new insights and inspiration for our own journeys through the wilderness.

BEMIDBAR

The desert is often seen as a barren wasteland, a place where life cannot thrive. But as the Torah teaches us, the desert is also a place of transformation and rebirth. In Bemidbar, we read about the journey of the Jewish People through the wilderness, as they traveled from Mount Sinai to the Promised Land. This journey was not easy, as they faced many challenges and obstacles along the way. But it was also a time of growth and transformation, as the people learned to rely on each other and on God.

In many ways, the rebirth of the Jewish People in the State of Israel is similar to the journey through the desert. Like the Israelites, we faced many challenges in the early years of the State, as we struggled to establish ourselves in a hostile region. We had to build a new society from scratch, while also defending ourselves from external threats. But like the Israelites, we also experienced a remarkable transformation, as we turned the desert into a thriving homeland for the Jewish People.

The key to this transformation was our willingness to take risks and to embrace new ideas. We had to be creative and innovative, to find ways to make the desert bloom. We invested in infrastructure and technology, in agriculture and industry, and we developed new ways of living and working that were uniquely suited to the desert environment.

But perhaps the most important lesson of the desert is the importance of community and unity. In the desert, the Israelites had to rely on each other for survival. They had to work together, to share their resources and to support each other through difficult times. This sense of community and unity was essential to their success, and it remains just as important for the State of Israel today.

As we face new challenges and opportunities in the 21st century, we must continue to draw inspiration from the journey of the Israelites through the desert. We must be willing to take risks, to embrace new ideas, and to work together to build a better future for ourselves and for our children. We must continue to invest in our infrastructure and our technology, to develop new industries and to explore new ways of living and working that are uniquely suited to the challenges of our time.

But above all, we must remain united as a people, and committed to the dream of a free and independent Jewish State. As I once said, "In Israel, in order to be a realist, you must believe in miracles." We have achieved many miracles in the past, and I am confident that we will continue to do so in the future. May we always be inspired by the lessons of the desert, and may we continue to build a strong and prosperous Israel for generations to come.

> DAVID BEN GURION WAS A ZIONIST LEADER WHO PLAYED A PIVOTAL ROLE IN THE ESTABLISHMENT OF THE STATE OF ISRAEL IN 1948. HE SERVED AS ISRAEL'S FIRST PRIME MINISTER AND WORKED TIRELESSLY TO BUILD THE COUNTRY'S POLITICAL AND MILITARY INSTITUTIONS.

In the Style of Georgia O'Keeffe

As I read Parashat Bemidbar, I am struck by the vivid descriptions of the desert landscape. The text speaks of the Israelites traveling through a "wilderness" and a "desolate place," where they are surrounded by sand, rocks, and harsh winds. This landscape is both barren and beautiful, with its stark simplicity and endless expanse.

I am drawn to the abstract shapes and colors that make up this desert landscape. The sand dunes ripple and curve, their pale beige color blending seamlessly into the sky. The rocks jut out from the ground like sculptures, their rough surfaces creating a visual contrast to the smooth curves of the dunes.

I often zoom in on a particular object or detail, to create a sense of intimacy with the subject. Similarly, the text of Parashat Bemidbar focuses on the details of the landscape, describing the different types of rocks and the patterns of the sand. These details help to create a sense of immersion in the desert world.

There is also a sense of movement. The wind is a constant presence in the desert, shaping the sand and rocks over time. This movement is captured through the use of swirling brushstrokes and dynamic compositions.

Parashat Bemidbar and artwork capture the beauty and complexity of the desert landscape. They remind us that even in the midst of desolation and barrenness, there is still a sense of wonder and awe to be found in the natural world.

> Georgia O'Keeffe was an American artist known for her stunning depictions of flowers, landscapes, and other natural subjects. Her unique style and use of color continue to inspire artists around the world today.

In the Style of Dante Alighieri

Midway through the desert, I found myself in a place
Where the Israelites roamed, led by God's grace
Their tents dotted the sands, as far as the eye could see
And I, Dante, felt humbled, by their faith so free

For forty long years, they wandered this land
Led by a cloud in the day, and a fire so grand
Their journey was fraught with danger and strife
But they held on to hope, and clung to God's life

As I walked through the dunes, I saw a mirage appear
A vision of manna, that God did provide near
It sustained them in hunger, and kept them alive
For in this harsh wilderness, only God could provide

The desert, I learned, was a place of transformation
For it stripped away all, of one's pride and ambition
Here, the Israelites learned to trust in the divine
For without God's help, survival was not mine

But in this barren wasteland, there was also beauty
The stars shone so bright, that it lit up the duty
Of those who walked this land, to serve the Almighty
And fulfill his commandments, with actions so mighty

As I turned to leave, I saw a glimmer of light
And realized that the desert, was a metaphor so bright
For in the wilderness of life, we all must tread
And rely on God's grace, to keep us ahead.

Thus, as I left the desert behind
I felt humbled, and yet so inclined
To walk this path, with faith so strong
And know that with God's help, I can never go wrong.

Dante Alighieri was an Italian poet and writer, widely regarded as one of the greatest poets in the Italian language and one of the most important figures in world literature. He is best known for his epic poem, The Divine Comedy, which is considered a masterpiece of world literature.

NASO

In the style of Bahya ibn Paquda

In Parashat Naso, we are reminded of the importance of personal and communal purity, as well as the consequences of breaking these laws. As a follower of the Jewish faith, I find myself drawn to the asceticism that is espoused in this parashat.

Asceticism is the act of voluntarily refraining from the pleasures and indulgences of the physical world, in order to focus on the spiritual. It is a practice that is intended to purify the body and soul, and to bring one closer to the divine.

Throughout Parashat Naso, we see examples of asceticism in the form of the Nazirite vow, which involves abstaining from wine, cutting one's hair, and avoiding contact with the dead. This vow is taken voluntarily, as a way of dedicating oneself to God, and is seen as a way to elevate oneself above the physical world.

As I reflect on this parashah, I am struck by the idea that asceticism is not just a matter of denying oneself physical pleasures, but of actively seeking out spiritual fulfillment. It is a reminder that the pursuit of material wealth and worldly pleasures can often distract us from our true purpose in life.

At the same time, I also recognize the challenges of living an ascetic lifestyle. It requires a great deal of discipline and self-control, as well as a willingness to forgo many of the comforts and pleasures that most people take for granted.

Yet, even as I acknowledge these challenges, I also see the potential rewards of asceticism. By purifying our bodies and souls, we can cultivate a deeper connection with the divine, and experience a sense of peace and fulfillment that is difficult to find in the material world.

In conclusion, Parashat Naso reminds us of the importance of spiritual purification, and offers a model for achieving this through asceticism. As we seek to navigate the challenges of life, let us strive to find a balance between the physical and spiritual, and to cultivate a deeper connection with the divine.

> Bahya ibn Paquda was a medieval Jewish philosopher and writer who lived in Spain. He is best known for his influential work "Duties of the Heart," which explores the inner spiritual and ethical dimensions of Judaism.

IN THE STYLE OF SUSAN B. ANTHONY

As I reflect on Parashat Naso and the concept of Sotah, I am reminded of the importance of a woman's personal dignity. In the Torah, the ritual of the Sotah was designed to address suspicion and doubts about a woman's fidelity, but it also reveals the patriarchal nature of the society in which it was written.

As a woman who dedicated her life to fighting for women's rights and suffrage, I believe that a woman's dignity should never be questioned or diminished. The Sotah ritual may have been a way to maintain order in ancient Israel, but it also reinforces the idea that women were seen as property to be controlled and managed by men.

In our modern times, we must continue to fight against any notion that would undermine the dignity and autonomy of women. We must work towards creating a society that values and respects the inherent worth of each individual, regardless of gender. Women have the right to live with dignity and respect, free from the judgment and suspicion of others.

As I reflect on Parashat Naso and the Sotah, I am reminded that we must continue to work towards a society that values women as equals, with the same rights and privileges as men. We must fight against any notion that seeks to diminish the worth and dignity of women, and work towards a world where all people are treated with respect and dignity.

> SUSAN B. ANTHONY WAS A WOMEN'S RIGHTS ACTIVIST, SUFFRAGIST, AND ABOLITIONIST WHO FOUGHT FOR GENDER AND RACIAL EQUALITY IN THE UNITED STATES. SHE WAS INSTRUMENTAL IN SECURING THE RIGHT TO VOTE FOR WOMEN THROUGH THE 19TH AMENDMENT TO THE U.S. CONSTITUTION.

IN THE STYLE OF ROBERT BELLAH

Parashat Naso marks a significant turning point in the evolution of religious leadership within the Jewish tradition. In this text, we see the emergence of the priestly class, who are designated as the primary religious leaders of the Israelite community.

Religion is not just a set of beliefs and practices but also a system of social organization, in which leadership plays a crucial role.

The focus on the priestly class in Parashat Naso is an example of this. The priests are designated as the mediators between the people and God, responsible for performing the sacrifices and other religious rituals. They are given a special role and status within the community, and their descendants are designated as the hereditary priests.

This development in Jewish religious leadership is significant because it represents a shift from a more egalitarian model to one that is more hierarchical. Before the priestly class emerged, religious leadership was shared by the elders of the community. However, with the establishment of the priests as the primary religious leaders, a new form of religious hierarchy emerged.

This evolution in religious leadership reflects the broader social and political changes taking place within the Israelite community. As the community became more centralized and urbanized, there was a need for a more formalized system of religious leadership. The emergence of the priestly class fulfilled this need, providing a stable and reliable source of religious authority.

In reflecting on Parashat Naso and the evolution of religious leadership within the Jewish tradition, we can see how religion is not static but rather evolves in response to changing social and political circumstances. Religion is not just a set of beliefs and practices but also a system of social organization, and the development of religious leadership reflects this.

> ROBERT BELLAH (1927-2013) WAS AN AMERICAN SOCIOLOGIST AND AUTHOR, KNOWN FOR HIS INFLUENTIAL WORKS ON RELIGION AND SOCIETY, INCLUDING "HABITS OF THE HEART" AND "RELIGION IN HUMAN EVOLUTION".

BE'HA'ALOTECHA

IN THE STYLE OF SIR ISAAC NEWTON

The image of the menorah in the Tabernacle, with its seven branches, evokes the seven colors of the spectrum that I discovered through my experiments with prisms.

Just as the menorah was a symbol of light in the Tabernacle, the spectrum of light is a symbol of the wondrous diversity of nature. The colors of the spectrum blend seamlessly into each other, like the branches of the menorah, yet each color is distinct and unique.

In my study of light, I discovered that white light is actually a combination of all the colors of the spectrum. The menorah, with its seven branches, represents this unity in diversity.

But just as the menorah had to be tended to and maintained, the spectrum of light requires careful attention and study. It is through our investigation and exploration of the natural world that we come to understand its secrets and beauty.

As I reflect on Parashat Beha'alotecha and the menorah, I am reminded of the importance of curiosity, inquiry, and exploration in our understanding of the world around us. Like the branches of the menorah, each discovery adds to the richness and complexity of our knowledge, and we must continually strive to expand our understanding of the world and its wonders.

> SIR ISAAC NEWTON (1642-1727) WAS AN ENGLISH PHYSICIST AND MATHEMATICIAN WHO IS WIDELY REGARDED AS ONE OF THE MOST INFLUENTIAL SCIENTISTS OF ALL TIME, KNOWN FOR HIS LAWS OF MOTION, CALCULUS, AND THEORY OF GRAVITATION. HIS DISCOVERIES AND CONTRIBUTIONS TO SCIENCE AND MATHEMATICS CONTINUE TO IMPACT OUR WORLD TODAY.

In Parashat Behaalotecha, we see a clear example of the importance of delegation and the challenges that come with it. Moses, the leader of the Israelites, is faced with the daunting task of leading a large group of people through the desert. In this parashah, we see how Moses grapples with the challenge of delegation, and we can draw valuable lessons from his experiences.

One of the key lessons that we can learn from Moses is the importance of selecting the right people for the job. When the Israelites complain about their lack of meat, Moses becomes overwhelmed and asks God to help him carry the burden. God advises Moses to select 70 elders to share in the responsibility of leading the people. Moses carefully chooses the 70 elders, making sure that they are capable and trustworthy individuals. This selection process is critical, as it ensures that the right people are in place to handle the task at hand.

Once the elders are selected, Moses delegates some of his responsibilities to them. This delegation allows Moses to focus on his most important tasks while empowering the elders to take on more responsibilities. However, we see that delegation is not always easy. Two of the elders, Eldad and Medad, begin prophesying outside the camp, and Joshua asks Moses to stop them. Moses responds by saying, "Are you jealous for my sake? Would that all the Lord's people were prophets, that the Lord would put his spirit upon them!" (Numbers 11:29). Moses recognizes that he cannot do everything himself, and that it is important to allow others to use their skills and talents to contribute to the community.

Another lesson we can learn from Moses is the importance of setting clear expectations and providing support. When Moses delegates responsibilities to the elders, he is careful to provide clear instructions on what is expected of them. He also provides support by ensuring that the elders have access to the resources and information they need to do their jobs effectively. This support is crucial in ensuring that the elders are successful in their new roles.

Finally, we see that delegation is not a one-time event. Moses continues to delegate responsibilities throughout his leadership of the Israelites, recognizing that delegation is an ongoing process. As the community grows and evolves, so too must the delegation of responsibilities.

In conclusion, Parashat Behaalotecha provides valuable lessons on the challenges and benefits of delegation. Moses serves as a model for effective delegation, demonstrating the importance of selecting the right people, setting clear expectations, providing support, and recognizing that delegation is an ongoing process. These lessons are relevant not only to leaders of religious communities but to leaders in all walks of life, and can help us build more effective and successful organizations. As I've said, "The leaders who work most effectively, it seems to me, never say 'I.' And that's not because they have trained themselves not to say 'I.' They don't think 'I.' They think 'we'; they think 'team.' They understand their job to be to make the team function. They accept responsibility and don't sidestep it, but 'we' gets the credit... This is what creates trust, what enables you to get the task done."

> PETER DRUCKER WAS A RENOWNED MANAGEMENT CONSULTANT, EDUCATOR, AND AUTHOR WHO IS WIDELY REGARDED AS THE FATHER OF MODERN MANAGEMENT THEORY. HE IS KNOWN FOR HIS INNOVATIVE IDEAS AND CONTRIBUTIONS TO THE FIELDS OF BUSINESS AND MANAGEMENT.

IN THE STYLE OF PAUL FARMER

Parashat Behaalotecha tells the story of Miriam's leprosy. Miriam, the sister of Moses and Aaron, is struck with a skin disease as punishment for speaking ill of her brother's wife. The Torah states that Moses cries out to God, "Please God, heal her" (Numbers 12:13), and after a week of quarantine, Miriam is cured.

This biblical tale, although ancient, has much to teach us about pragmatic solidarity and communal health. Health and illness are not solely individual experiences. Rather, they are intimately tied to the social, economic, and political structures that govern our lives.

In the case of Miriam's leprosy, her illness not only affected her but also put the entire community at risk. Leprosy, also known as Hansen's disease, is a highly contagious bacterial infection that can cause disfiguration, nerve damage, and blindness if left untreated. Therefore, in the interest of communal health, Miriam had to be isolated and treated.

Moses' cry for healing is an example of pragmatic solidarity, a concept that I've described as "an ethics of shared action, mutual responsibility, and interdependence." Moses did not abandon his sister to her illness but instead worked to ensure that she received the care she needed. This type of solidarity is essential in promoting health and well-being in communities.

Additionally, the story of Miriam's leprosy highlights the importance of addressing the social and cultural factors that contribute to illness. Miriam's punishment for speaking ill of her sister-in-law suggests that the disease was not solely biological but also had a cultural component. In this case, Miriam's disrespect for her sister-in-law may have reflected larger societal prejudices against the Cushite tribe.

Addressing these social and cultural factors is essential in promoting health equity. To truly address the root causes of illness, we must look beyond the individual level and consider the larger social and political context in which illness occurs.

In conclusion, the story of Miriam's leprosy offers a powerful lesson in pragmatic solidarity and communal health. As we work to promote health and well-being in our communities, we must remember that health is not solely an individual experience but is intimately tied to the social, economic, and political structures that govern our lives. By working together, we can address the root causes of illness and promote health equity for all.

PAUL FARMER WAS AN AMERICAN MEDICAL ANTHROPOLOGIST AND PHYSICIAN, WIDELY RECOGNIZED FOR HIS WORK IN GLOBAL HEALTH. HE WAS THE CO-FOUNDER OF PARTNERS IN HEALTH AND A PROFESSOR AT HARVARD MEDICAL SCHOOL.

SHLACH

IN THE STYLE OF THE CHILDLIKE EMPRESS

I have seen many stories unfold throughout time, some happy, and some sad. One of the stories that I remember well is Parashat Shlach, a Torah portion that speaks of hope for the future.

The story tells of the twelve spies that were sent to explore the land of Canaan, the Promised Land that was meant to be the home of the Israelites. But when the spies returned, ten of them brought back a negative report, causing the Israelites to lose faith in their future.

It is easy to lose hope when things do not go as planned. But I have learned that hope is the key to overcoming any challenge. When the Israelites lost faith, it was Joshua and Caleb who remained hopeful, even in the face of adversity. They refused to give up on their dream of a better future, and it was their hope that eventually led the Israelites to the Promised Land.

For me, Parashat Shlach is a reminder that hope is a powerful force that can change the course of history. It is easy to give up when things are difficult, but hope gives us the strength to keep going, even when the road ahead seems long and uncertain.

In the Neverending Story, hope is what saves the magical world of Fantasia from being consumed by the Nothing. It is the hope of the young hero, Atreyu, that ultimately brings him to me, where he learns that he is the only one who can save the world he loves.

Like Atreyu, the Israelites were able to find hope in the midst of despair. I believe that hope is the key to a better future for all of us. No matter what challenges we face, hope can give us the strength to keep moving forward, one step at a time.

So let us all be like Joshua and Caleb, and hold on to hope, even in the face of adversity. Let us remember that the future is always full of possibilities, and that with hope, we can create a better world for ourselves and for those around us.

> THE CHILDLIKE EMPRESS IS THE MYTHICAL RULER OF FANTASIA, A REALM OF INFINITE POSSIBILITIES IN THE NOVEL THE NEVERENDING STORY. SHE IS THE EMBODIMENT OF PURENESS AND HOPE, AND HER POWER LIES IN THE IMAGINATION OF THOSE WHO BELIEVE IN HER.

As a student of Moshe Rabbeinu and a leader of the Jewish people, I have learned the importance of observation in our journey towards the Promised Land. This lesson is exemplified in Parashat Shlach, which tells the story of the twelve spies who were sent to scout the land of Canaan.

The mission of the spies was to bring back a report on the land, its people, and its resources. However, ten of the spies focused on the negative aspects of the land, highlighting the strong fortifications and powerful armies of the Canaanites. They saw only obstacles and challenges, and their report discouraged the people, causing them to lose faith in God and His promise of the land.

In contrast, my fellow spy Caleb and I took a different approach. We observed the same land and the same people, but we saw things from a different perspective. We focused on the positive aspects of the land, its abundance and fertility, and we were confident that with God's help we could conquer it.

Our ability to observe and interpret what we saw allowed us to remain faithful to God and to our mission. It was a lesson in the art of observation, a skill that is critical to our success as a people and as individuals.

As I reflect on this story, I am reminded of the importance of observation in our daily lives. Just as we needed to observe the land of Canaan and interpret what we saw in order to succeed, we must observe the world around us and make wise decisions based on our observations.

Observation is not a passive act; it requires an active and discerning mind. It requires us to focus on the details, to be aware of our biases and assumptions, and to be open to new perspectives. It requires us to seek the truth, even when it may be difficult or uncomfortable.

As we navigate the challenges of life, we must remember the lesson of Parashat Shlach. We must observe our surroundings, interpret what we see, and make wise decisions based on our observations. We must have the courage to see things from a different perspective and the faith to believe that with God's help, we can overcome any obstacle.

In conclusion, the art of observation is a critical skill that we must cultivate in order to succeed in life. We can learn from the example of Caleb and I in Parashat Shlach, who saw the same land as the other spies but interpreted it differently. May we have the wisdom and discernment to observe the world around us and make wise decisions that lead us towards a life of purpose and fulfillment.

> Yehoshua ben Nun was a prominent figure in Jewish history, known for his leadership during the conquest of Canaan. He succeeded Moses as the leader of the Israelites.

In the style of Rebecca

As I reflect on Parashat Shlach, I am reminded of the courage it takes to make difficult choices about the future. As a biblical figure, I know all too well the importance of taking risks, standing up for what you believe in, and facing the unknown with confidence and faith.

In this week's Torah portion, we read about the twelve spies who were sent to explore the land of Canaan. When they returned, they reported that the land was bountiful, but also filled with danger and opposition. Ten of the spies were filled with fear and doubt, and discouraged the Israelites from entering the land. Only two, Joshua and Caleb, had the courage to see beyond the challenges and focus on the potential rewards.

As I reflect on this story, I am reminded of my own difficult choices in life. When my husband Isaac was preparing to bless his son Esau, I knew that he was making a grave mistake. I had faith that our son Jacob was the right choice to receive the blessing, and I was willing to take a risk to make sure that he did. I knew that the consequences of my actions could be severe, but I had the courage to stand up for what I believed in.

Like Joshua and Caleb, I was willing to face the unknown and take a risk. I knew that the future was uncertain, but I had faith that things would work out in the end. And indeed, my actions led to the fulfillment of God's plan for our family and our people.

In today's world, we face many challenges and uncertainties. We must make difficult choices about the future, both for ourselves and for our communities. But we must remember the lessons of Parashat Shlach, and have the courage to face these challenges with faith and determination.

We must be like Joshua and Caleb, who saw the potential in the land of Canaan and were willing to take a risk to make it their own. We must conjure the courage to stand up for what is right, even when the consequences are uncertain.

Let us be inspired by these biblical figures, and let us have the courage to make difficult choices about the future, with faith and determination. May we be blessed with the strength and courage to face any challenge that comes our way.

Amen.

> Rebecca was a prominent figure in the book of Genesis, known for her beauty, kindness, and unwavering faith in God. She was the wife of Isaac and the mother of Jacob and Esau.

KORACH

IN THE STYLES OF DATAN AND AVIRAM

As we reflect on Parashat Korach, we are reminded of the dangers of mob mentality and the consequences that can come from following the wrong leader. We are Datam and Aviram, two individuals who were involved in this story, and we would like to share our perspectives on this important topic.

At the heart of the story of Korach is the issue of leadership. Korach and his followers were challenging the authority of Moses and Aaron, claiming that they were no more deserving of leadership than anyone else in the community. They argued that everyone should have an equal say in the decisions that affected the community as a whole.

As we look back on this story, we can see that Korach and his followers were not acting out of a genuine concern for the welfare of the community. Rather, they were motivated by their own desire for power and influence. They saw an opportunity to challenge Moses and Aaron and to promote their own agenda, and they took it.

This is where the danger of mob mentality comes in. When a group of people get together and become caught up in a particular idea or ideology, they can lose sight of the bigger picture. They can become so focused on their own goals and desires that they fail to consider the needs of the community as a whole. This is what happened with Korach and his followers. They became so convinced of their own rightness that they failed to see the damage they were causing.

As individuals who were involved in this story, we can attest to the fact that it is easy to get caught up in the energy and excitement of a crowd. It is easy to go along with what everyone else is saying and to ignore your own doubts and reservations. But this is where we need to be careful. We need to be aware of the potential dangers of mob mentality and to resist the temptation to go along with the crowd.

In conclusion, the story of Korach serves as a powerful reminder of the dangers of mob mentality and the importance of choosing our leaders wisely. As individuals, we must be careful not to get swept up in the energy of a crowd and to always remember the bigger picture. We must be willing to speak up and to challenge ideas that we believe are harmful or misguided. Only then can we ensure that our communities are guided by leaders who truly have the best interests of all members in mind.

> DATAN AND AVIRAM WERE TWO ISRAELITE MEN WHO REBELLED AGAINST MOSES AND AARON, LEADING A FACTION OF THE COMMUNITY THAT OPPOSED THEIR LEADERSHIP. THEY WERE ULTIMATELY PUNISHED BY GOD FOR THEIR DISOBEDIENCE.

In the style of Mercy Otis Warren

In Parashat Korach, we are presented with a story of rebellion against Moses and Aaron's leadership among the Israelites. The rebellion is led by Korach, a Levite who challenges the authority of Moses and Aaron, arguing that all the people are holy and should have equal access to the priesthood. This rebellion is one of many that have occurred throughout history, and it is important to understand the different kinds of rebellions that exist.

As I once said, "Rebellion against tyrants is obedience to God." This statement highlights the notion that rebellion can be a necessary and justified response to oppressive leadership. However, not all rebellions are created equal, and it is important to distinguish between them.

The rebellion of Korach in Parashat Korach can be categorized as a power struggle rebellion. This type of rebellion is motivated by a desire for power and control, and it often involves challenging the existing leadership structure. In the case of Korach, he is dissatisfied with his position as a Levite and seeks to elevate himself to the position of a priest. Korach's rebellion ultimately fails, as Moses and Aaron are able to demonstrate that they have been chosen by God to lead the people.

Another type of rebellion is the social justice rebellion. This type of rebellion is motivated by a desire to address social and economic inequality. It often involves marginalized groups challenging the status quo and demanding equal rights and opportunities. An example of this type of rebellion is the civil rights movement in the United States, where African Americans challenged the institutionalized racism that permeated American society.

A third type of rebellion is the ideological rebellion. This type of rebellion is motivated by a desire to challenge and overthrow an oppressive ideology. It often involves challenging the prevailing political or religious beliefs of a society. The French Revolution is an example of this type of rebellion, where the people of France challenged the oppressive monarchical system and sought to establish a more egalitarian and democratic society.

In conclusion, the rebellion of Korach in Parashat Korach is just one example of the many rebellions that have occurred throughout history. By distinguishing between the different types of rebellions, we can better understand the motivations and goals of those who challenge the status quo. It is important to remember that rebellion can be a powerful tool for achieving social justice and freedom, but it must be used judiciously and with care. Yes, rebellion against tyrants is obedience to God, but it is up to us to determine when and how to rebel.

Mercy Otis Warren was a prominent writer and political commentator during the American Revolution.

In the style of Rabbi Everett Gendler

Shalom, my dear friends,

As we study Parashat Korach, we are confronted with a stark reminder of the human capacity to contaminate the earth, both physically and spiritually. In this portion, we see Korach and his followers rebel against Moses and Aaron, and in doing so, they bring about destruction and chaos.

We can see the parallels between Korach's rebellion and the ways in which humans have been polluting the earth for centuries. Just as Korach's actions led to a rupture in the community, the impact of human pollution on the environment has caused significant damage to our planet and its inhabitants.

But what can we learn from this parashah? How can we draw upon its lessons to create a more sustainable and just world?

First and foremost, we must recognize that our actions have consequences. We cannot continue to ignore the impact that our choices have on the environment and on other living beings. We must take responsibility for our actions and work to mitigate the harm that we have caused.

Secondly, we must resist the temptation to place ourselves above others. Korach's rebellion was rooted in his desire for power and recognition, and we see this same impulse in the way that humans have exploited and mistreated the earth and its inhabitants for our own benefit.

Finally, we must acknowledge the interconnectedness of all living beings. Just as Korach's rebellion affected the entire community, our actions affect the health and well-being of all living things. We must work to cultivate a deep sense of empathy and interconnectedness with the world around us, and strive to live in harmony with the natural world.

As Rabbi Heschel once said, "In a free society where bad habits are tolerated, the atmosphere is poisoned by disbelief, cynicism and corruption." We must not tolerate the bad habits of pollution, but rather work to create a society that values the health and well-being of all living things.

May we learn from the lessons of Parashat Korach and work to create a world that is just, sustainable, and in harmony with the natural world.

Shalom.

Rabbi Everett Gendler was an influential American rabbi, activist, and social justice advocate who played a significant role in the Civil Rights Movement of the 1960s.

CHUKAT

In the style of Emily Dickinson

In Israel's desert land of old,
The faithful people roamed.
With Miriam there to lead the way,
Their journey brightly shone.

But on the day when Miriam died,
The people mourned her loss.
A prophetess of highest rank,
She paid the mortal cost.

The well that had sustained them all,
Dried up upon her death.
And all the people, parched with thirst,
Were left with bated breath.

For forty years she'd been their guide,
Their beacon in the night.
And now that she had left their midst,
The people lost their sight.

No more would Miriam dance and sing,
Or play her tambourine.
No more would she be there to help
Them when they needed it.

The people, lost without her light,
Began to wander aimlessly.
With no direction, they fell prey
To hunger and to strife.

But in the darkest of their days,
A miracle occurred.
For on the day when Miriam died,
A new well did emerge.

And from its depths, the people drank,
Revived by Miriam's love.
For even though her body's gone,
Her spirit still lives on.

Her memory's a guiding star,
That lights their way to peace.
And every time they hear her name,
Their hope and faith increase.

For Miriam was a prophetess,
A woman pure and true.
And though her death was hard to bear,
Her legacy lives through.

So let us all remember her,
And all that she has done.
For Miriam's life was full of love,
And through her, we have won.

Emily Dickinson was an American poet known for her unique style and themes of nature, death, and spirituality.

IN THE STYLE OF JOAN DIDION

In Parashat Chukat, we are presented with a complex and emotionally charged moment in the life of Moses, the great leader of the Israelites. The passage describes how Moses, in the wake of his sister Miriam's death, struggles to come to terms with his grief and his feelings of powerlessness in the face of God's will. This inner turmoil ultimately leads him to commit a grave error, striking a rock in anger and disobeying God's command. I will explore the profound themes of loss, grief, and human fallibility that emerge from this powerful story.

The story of Moses and the rock is a stark reminder of the fragility of human emotions and the destructive power of grief. We see how Moses, despite his great wisdom and leadership, is vulnerable to the same fears and doubts that afflict all of us. His grief for his sister Miriam is overwhelming, and he is struggling to reconcile himself to her death. As he leads the Israelites through the desert, his sense of isolation and loneliness is palpable, and he becomes increasingly disconnected from the people he is supposed to guide.

Moses' anger and frustration finally come to a head when God instructs him to speak to a rock in order to provide water for the Israelites. In a moment of emotional turmoil, Moses lashes out, striking the rock in anger and disobeying God's command. This act of rebellion has grave consequences, and Moses is denied the chance to lead the Israelites into the promised land.

Moses' struggle with grief and loss is a universal human experience. We all face the prospect of losing those we love, and we must all learn to cope with the pain and confusion that comes with such a loss. The story of Moses reminds us that even the greatest among us can be brought low by the weight of our emotions, and that the line between rationality and irrationality is a thin one.

At the same time, the story of Moses and the rock also offers a message of hope. Despite his moment of weakness, Moses remains a towering figure in Jewish tradition, revered for his wisdom, strength, and devotion to God. We see that even in the face of tragedy and grief, there is the possibility of redemption and renewal. The rock may have been struck, but the waters of faith continue to flow.

In conclusion, the story of Moses and the rock is a powerful meditation on the human experience of loss and grief. We can see how this story speaks to universal themes of emotion and fallibility, while also offering a message of hope and resilience. As we confront the challenges of our own lives, may we draw strength from the example of Moses and the wisdom of our tradition.

> Joan Didion was a renowned American writer, known for her distinctive style of journalism and insightful essays on culture and politics.

In the Style of the Red Heifer

They say I'm holy, and that's all fine,
But let me tell you, it's quite a grind,
Being a red heifer is a state of mind.

I'm the red heifer, and I'm quite rare,
People flock to see me from everywhere,
I can't help but wonder, do they even care?

I'm the red heifer, I'm not a clown,
But sometimes I feel like the talk of the town,
I guess that's what happens when you're holy and brown.

They say I'm pure, without any sin,
But let me tell you, it's not easy being in,
The red heifer business, it's a hard road to begin.

I'm the red heifer, the chosen one,
But sometimes I wish I could just have some fun,
Like grazing in the fields, or soaking up the sun.

They call me special, and that's just fine,
But I'm just a cow, not divine,
So let's move on, and talk about something benign.

The Red Heifer is a biblical figure, known for its rarity.

BALAK

My brothers and sisters, hear me, for I have a story to tell of dreams and prophecy, of a man named Bilaam and the king who sought his services. This tale comes from the Book of Numbers, in the portion known as Balak, where we find Bilaam, a non-Israelite prophet, sought out by the king of Moab to curse the Israelite people.

But Bilaam, like me, was a dreamer. He received visions from the divine, and it was in these dreams that he was able to discern the true will of the Holy One. And so, when the king of Moab came to him and offered him great riches in exchange for his services, Bilaam had a dream that warned him not to go with the king's messengers.

But the king was persistent, and so Bilaam had another dream, in which the divine messenger granted him permission to go with the king, but with the strict condition that he speak only the words that the divine messenger would give him.

And so, Bilaam set out with the king's messengers, but along the way, his donkey saw an angel of the divine blocking their path. Bilaam, blinded by his desire for wealth and power, did not see the angel, but his donkey did, and so the donkey refused to move forward.

In his anger, Bilaam struck the donkey, and it was then that the divine messenger appeared to him, rebuking him for his cruelty and reminding him of his duty to speak only the words that were given to him.

Bilaam, humbled and repentant, went with the king to curse the Israelites, but every time he opened his mouth to curse, he was instead filled with blessings for the people of Israel.

In the end, Bilaam's dreams and visions revealed the truth to him, that the Israelites were a blessed people, chosen by the divine, and that no curse could ever bring harm to them.

My brothers and sisters, this story teaches us the importance of listening to the divine, of heeding the messages we receive in our dreams and visions, and of recognizing the sacredness of all life, even that of a humble donkey. Let us take heed of Bilaam's example, and strive to use our dreams and visions for the good of all.

JOSEPH WAS AN IMPORTANT FIGURE IN THE TORAHG, KNOWN FOR HIS COLORFUL COAT, HIS INTERPRETATION OF DREAMS, AND HIS RISE TO POWER IN EGYPT. HE IS ALSO REMEMBERED FOR HIS FORGIVENESS TOWARDS HIS BROTHERS WHO HAD SOLD HIM INTO SLAVERY.

In the style of the Talking Donkey

A talking donkey would grab anyone's attention, right? Well, let me tell you, as a talking donkey myself, it's not always as exciting as it sounds. But when I look back on my experience, I realize that it wasn't all bad. I mean, I did get to talk to a prophet, and that's not something you can say every day. And hey, I even managed to save my owner's life while I was at it.

But let's start from the beginning. I was just your average donkey, living a normal donkey life, eating hay and carrying loads, when one day my owner, Balaam, decided to take me on a journey to see the king of Moab. I was just minding my own business, munching on some hay, when all of a sudden, an angel appeared in front of me. And what do you know, I suddenly found myself speaking the same language as my owner.

Now, I know what you're thinking. A talking donkey? That's crazy, right? But trust me, it was just as crazy for me as it was for Balaam. But as we journeyed on, I realized that my newfound ability to speak was not just for show. It was a gift that was given to me so that I could help my owner avoid danger and destruction.

You see, the king of Moab had hired Balaam to curse the Israelites, who were on their way to the Promised Land. But as we made our way toward the Israelites, I sensed that something wasn't right. I tried to steer Balaam off the path, but he wouldn't listen. And that's when the angel appeared to me, blocking our way.

Balaam couldn't see the angel, but I could, and I knew that we were in danger. So, I spoke up, and what do you know, Balaam actually listened to me. We managed to avoid disaster, and Balaam realized that I wasn't just an ordinary donkey, but a special one, chosen by God to speak to him and protect him from harm.

Now, I know what you're thinking. This story sounds a lot like the plot of that movie Shrek. And you're right, it does. But let me tell you, being a talking donkey is nothing like that. For one, we don't eat parfaits all day long. And as for that boulder, well, let's just say that it's not something I care to remember.

But in all seriousness, my experience taught me a valuable lesson. Sometimes, the most unexpected things can happen, and we have to be open to them. We might not understand why they're happening, but we have to trust that there's a purpose and a plan behind it all. And who knows, maybe we'll even learn something from it in the end.

So, there you have it, my friends. The story of the talking donkey from "Parashat Balak." It may sound a bit far-fetched, but trust me, it's a story worth telling. And as for me, well, let's just say that I'm happy to be back to my normal donkey life, eating hay and carrying loads, and leaving the talking to the humans.

> BALAAM'S TALKING DONKEY IS A NOTABLE CHARACTER IN THE BOOK OF NUMBERS, KNOWN FOR ITS MIRACULOUS ABILITY TO SPEAK TO BALAAM AND CONVEY GOD'S MESSAGE. THIS DONKEY SERVES AS A MESSENGER OF DIVINE TRUTH, CHALLENGING BALAAM'S PRIDE AND ARROGANCE.

IN THE STYLE OF DONKEY FROM SHREK

Hello there! It's me, Donkey from Shrek, and I'm here to talk to you about a very special donkey that I heard about in the Torah. Yes, you heard me right, there's another talking donkey in town, and his name is... well, actually, we don't know his name, but he appears in Parashat Balak.

Now, this donkey is quite the character. He's owned by a man named Balaam, who's not the nicest guy around. In fact, he's been hired by the king of Moab to curse the Israelites, who are passing through his land. But this donkey, he's got a mind of his own. When Balaam starts hitting him, the donkey speaks up and says, "What have I done to you, that you have beaten me these three times?"

And here's where things get really interesting. Balaam, who's never heard a donkey talk before, doesn't even seem surprised. He just starts arguing with the donkey, and the two of them have a full-blown conversation about why the donkey stopped walking.

As a talking donkey myself, I have to say, I'm impressed by this guy. Not only does he have the gift of gab, but he's also got some serious guts. He's standing up to his abusive owner and speaking truth to power, even though he knows it could mean trouble for him.

And it turns out, this donkey is more than just a chatterbox. He's actually got some serious prophetic powers. Later on in the story, he sees an angel of God blocking their path, while Balaam is too blinded by his own greed to notice. The donkey turns off the path and ends up saving Balaam's life.

Now, I don't know about you, but I think this donkey is a hero. He's not afraid to speak up for what's right, even when it's risky or unpopular. And he's got a special gift, one that he uses to help others and protect them from danger.

So, what can we learn from this talking donkey in Parashat Balak? Well, for starters, we can remember to speak up when we see injustice or cruelty. We can use our voices to defend the vulnerable and stand up for what's right, even if it means going against the crowd.

And we can also remember that sometimes, the most unexpected heroes can come in the most unexpected forms. Who would have thought that a donkey could save a man's life, or that he could be a messenger of God's will?

So let's give it up for the donkey in Parashat Balak, and all the other unexpected heroes out there. You never know where you might find courage, wisdom, or the power of speech. And who knows, maybe one day you'll hear a donkey like me talking in the Torah too. Stranger things have happened, right?

Until then, keep on talking, keep on standing up for what's right, and keep on believing in the power of the unexpected. Thanks for listening, folks. It's been a real pleasure.

> The talking donkey in Shrek is a witty and lovable companion who never fails to make audiences laugh with his hilarious antics and quick comebacks.

PINCHAS

IN THE STYLE OF ETHEL SNOWDEN

The story of Parashat Pinchas in the book of Numbers is one that has caused much debate and controversy over the years. It tells the story of a young man named Pinchas who, in a fit of zealotry, kills an Israelite man and a Midianite woman who were engaging in sexual relations. While some have interpreted this act as an act of heroism, others have seen it as an example of the dangers of zealotry and violence.

As a pacifist and social activist, I firmly believe that violence is never the answer. While it may seem justified in the heat of the moment, it ultimately only leads to more pain and suffering. In the case of Pinchas, his actions may have seemed righteous to him, but they ultimately caused harm to both himself and those around him.

Moreover, the story of Parashat Pinchas is a warning against the dangers of zealotry. When we become too passionate about our beliefs, we can easily lose sight of our compassion and empathy. We may feel justified in our actions, but in reality, we are only causing more harm than good.

I would urge all those who read this story to take it as a cautionary tale. We must be careful not to let our passions and convictions cloud our judgment, and we must always strive to act with compassion and understanding. Only by working together and embracing our shared humanity can we hope to build a better and more just world.

In the end, the story of Parashat Pinchas is not one of heroism, but of the dangers of zealotry and violence. We must all take it as a reminder of the importance of peace and empathy, and work together to create a better world for all.

ETHEL SNOWDEN (1881-1951) WAS A BRITISH POLITICIAN, FEMINIST, AND PACIFIST WHO PLAYED A KEY ROLE IN THE EARLY YEARS OF THE BRITISH LABOUR PARTY. SHE WAS THE FIRST WOMAN TO SERVE AS A LABOUR MEMBER OF PARLIAMENT IN THE HOUSE OF COMMONS.

Parashat Pinchas is a story that presents us with the dangers of religious extremism. In this story, we see a character named Pinchas, who zealously kills two people for engaging in sexual immorality, an act that was seen as a grave sin in the eyes of God. While some might view Pinchas as a hero, the truth is that his actions were not justified, and they serve as a warning to us all about the dangers of religious extremism.

In our modern world, we are surrounded by examples of religious extremism. From ISIS to the Westboro Baptist Church, there are countless examples of individuals and groups who take their beliefs to dangerous and violent extremes. The problem with religious extremism is that it often leads to a lack of empathy and understanding, as well as a disregard for the well-being of others.

Pinchas is a prime example of this lack of empathy. He saw the sin committed by the two people and reacted without considering the ramifications of his actions. While he may have believed that he was doing the right thing in the eyes of God, the truth is that he was causing harm to others and creating a rift within the community.

This is a problem that we see in many religious extremist groups today. They may believe that they are doing the right thing in the eyes of their god or gods, but their actions often cause harm and suffering to others. They become so focused on their beliefs that they lose sight of the humanity of those around them.

Another danger of religious extremism is that it can lead to a lack of progress and innovation. When individuals or groups become too focused on their beliefs and the way things have always been done, they can become resistant to change and progress. This can lead to a stagnation of ideas and a lack of growth within the community.

In the case of Pinchas, his actions created a divide within the community. Instead of working together to address the issue of sexual immorality, he took matters into his own hands and caused harm to others. This lack of cooperation and understanding is a danger that we see in many religious extremist groups today. They become so focused on their beliefs that they are unable to work with others to create positive change.

In conclusion, the story of Pinchas is a warning about the dangers of religious extremism. It shows us that when individuals or groups become too focused on their beliefs, they can lose sight of the humanity of those around them. This lack of empathy can lead to harm and suffering for others, as well as a lack of progress and growth within the community. As we move forward, we must be mindful of these dangers and work to promote understanding and cooperation within our communities. Only by doing so can we create a world that is truly inclusive and compassionate.

> Aviezer Ravitzky (1940-2013) was an Israeli philosopher, historian and theologian known for his expertise in Jewish philosophy and modern Jewish thought. His work focused on the intersection of religion, politics and society in Israel.

Parashat Pinchas is a complex and multi-layered text that touches on a variety of themes, including leadership, justice, and gender roles. As a physician, suffragist, and feminist, I am particularly interested in the place of women in this portion and how it speaks to the ongoing struggle for gender equality in our society.

One of the key events in Parashat Pinchas is the rebellion of Korah, Dathan, and Abiram, who challenge the authority of Moses and Aaron and claim that all the people are holy and worthy of leadership. In response, God punishes them by causing the earth to swallow them up. This episode raises important questions about the nature of leadership and who is entitled to wield it.

At the same time, the portion also contains a story about the daughters of Zelophehad, who approach Moses and ask for their father's inheritance, as he had no sons. Moses consults with God, who confirms that the daughters are entitled to the land and can pass it on to their descendants. This is a remarkable moment, as it represents a departure from the usual patriarchal inheritance laws and acknowledges the rights of women to property.

However, it is important to note that the daughters of Zelophehad are exceptional women, who are praised for their intelligence, courage, and devotion to God. They are not representative of the average woman in ancient Israel, who had limited opportunities for education, employment, and public participation. Moreover, the fact that they have to appeal to Moses and God for their rights highlights the fact that they are operating within a patriarchal system that does not recognize their full humanity.

This tension between the exceptional and the normative is reflected in other aspects of Parashat Pinchas as well. For example, the portion contains a census of the Israelites, which only includes men who are 20 years old and above. This exclusion of women and younger men from the count reinforces the idea that only certain people count as full members of the community, while others are seen as peripheral or inferior.

Similarly, the portion also deals with the issue of sacrifices and offerings, which are primarily performed by men and priests. Women are mentioned in this context only in relation to their menstrual cycle, which renders them impure and temporarily bars them from participating in certain rituals. This biological determinism reinforces the notion that women's bodies are inherently different and inferior to men's, and therefore women are not fully capable of engaging with the divine.

In conclusion, Parashat Pinchas presents a complex and nuanced view of the place of women in ancient Israelite society. While it contains moments of progress and recognition of women's rights, it also highlights the pervasive influence of patriarchal norms and structures. As we continue to fight for gender equality in our own time, we can draw inspiration from the daughters of Zelophehad and other women who challenged the status quo and demanded their rightful place in society. At the same time, we must remain vigilant against the subtle forms of exclusion and discrimination that still exist and work to create a world where all people are recognized as holy and worthy of leadership.

> MARY EDWARDS WALKER WAS A PHYSICIAN, ABOLITIONIST, AND WOMEN'S RIGHTS ACTIVIST WHO WAS THE FIRST WOMAN TO RECEIVE THE MEDAL OF HONOR. SHE DEDICATED HER LIFE TO FIGHTING FOR EQUALITY AND JUSTICE FOR ALL.

MATOT

In Parashat Matot, we find an intriguing tale of broken promises and the consequences that ensue. This story speaks to the human condition and highlights the struggle that we all face when it comes to fulfilling our commitments. As I once said, "We are all capable of betraying and hurting those we love."

In the Parashat Matot, Moses commands the Israelites to take vengeance on the Midianites for their role in seducing the Israelites into idolatry. The tribes of Reuben and Gad offer to fight on behalf of Israel but request that they be allowed to settle in the fertile lands of Gilead rather than the land of Canaan. Moses initially agrees to their request, but later he admonishes them for breaking their promise to fight alongside the other tribes until Canaan is conquered.

This story is a cautionary tale of the importance of keeping one's promises. The tribes of Reuben and Gad were initially praised for their offer to fight alongside their brothers. However, their failure to follow through on their commitment ultimately led to mistrust and division among the tribes.

Furthermore, this story illustrates the complexities of human nature. We are all capable of making promises that we cannot keep, and we are all capable of betraying those we love. Human beings are constantly struggling to find meaning in a world that is fundamentally meaningless. In this context, promises and commitments serve as a way for us to create order and structure in our lives. When we break these promises, we are essentially rejecting the order that we have created and returning to a state of chaos.

In Parashat Matot, Moses reminds us that our commitments are not to be taken lightly. Whether we are making promises to our friends, family, or colleagues, we must be willing to follow through on them if we hope to maintain trust and respect. Our ability to keep our promises is often hindered by our own weaknesses and flaws. However, it is through the struggle to keep our promises that we find meaning and purpose in our lives.

In conclusion, Parashat Matot and its story of broken promises serves as a powerful reminder of the importance of keeping our commitments. Whether we are making promises to ourselves or to others, we must be willing to follow through on them if we hope to find meaning and purpose in our lives. As I once said, "The only way to deal with fear is to face it head-on." Similarly, the only way to deal with our fear of failure when it comes to keeping our promises is to face it head-on and do our best to follow through on our commitments.

Albert Camus (1913-1960) was a French writer and philosopher known for his existentialist works, including the novel "The Stranger" and the essay "The Myth of Sisyphus". He was awarded the Nobel Prize in Literature in 1957.

IN THE STYLE OF PRESIDENT ABRAHAM LINCOLN

Dear Fellow Citizens,

As we reflect upon Parashat Matot, we are reminded of the importance of unity and solidarity within our communities. The division of tribes, as described in this portion, is a lesson that resonates with us even today.

I once said, "A house divided against itself cannot stand." The division of tribes in Parashat Matot serves as a cautionary tale about the dangers of disunity. The tribes of Reuben, Gad, and half of the tribe of Manasseh requested to settle on the east side of the Jordan River, away from the rest of the Israelites. While this request was granted, it created a sense of separation between the tribes.

Unity was essential for a society to prosper. We are stronger together than we are apart. Similarly, the division of the tribes in Parashat Matot weakened the Israelite community. It created a sense of distance between the tribes and made it difficult for them to come together and support one another.

Moreover, differences and disagreements were inevitable in any society. However, we should work to find common ground and strive for unity despite our differences. The division of the tribes in Parashat Matot was not based on disagreement or conflict, but rather on a desire for separation.

As we navigate the complexities of our own society, we must remember the importance of unity and solidarity. We must work to bridge the gaps between us and find common ground. We must embrace our differences and use them to strengthen us, rather than divide us.

In conclusion, the lessons of Parashat Matot remind us of the importance of unity and solidarity. We must work to come together as a community, despite our differences, and strive for a brighter future together. As I once said, "We are not enemies, but friends. We must not be enemies. Though passion may have strained it must not break our bonds of affection."

ABRAHAM LINCOLN WAS THE 16TH PRESIDENT OF THE UNITED STATES, SERVING FROM 1861 UNTIL HIS ASSASSINATION IN 1865. HE IS KNOWN FOR HIS LEADERSHIP DURING THE CIVIL WAR AND HIS EFFORTS TO ABOLISH SLAVERY.

IN THE STYLE OF DORIAN GRAY

As I reflect on Parashat Matot and the concept of annulment of vows, I cannot help but be reminded of my own experiences with promises and oaths. Like many individuals, I have made countless vows throughout my life – some of which I have kept, and others that I have broken. However, the Torah teaches us that there are times when it is permissible, and even necessary, to annul a vow. This idea of nullifying a promise is one that has fascinated me for years, as it raises questions about the true nature of our word and the power that it holds.

In my youth, I was known for my beauty and charm, and I used my charisma to manipulate and deceive those around me. I made promises that I had no intention of keeping, and swore oaths that I had no desire to fulfill. As a result, I became consumed by vanity and selfishness, and I lost sight of what truly mattered in life. However, as I grew older and faced the consequences of my actions, I began to understand the importance of keeping one's word.

Parashat Matot speaks of a person who makes a vow or oath, and later regrets it. The Torah states that in such a case, the individual may come before a court of law and ask for the vow to be annulled. The judges would then examine the circumstances surrounding the vow, and determine whether or not it should be nullified. This process of annulment was not taken lightly, as it acknowledged the gravity of one's word, while also recognizing the complexities of human nature.

As I reflect on this concept of annulment, I cannot help but feel a sense of empathy for those who have made promises that they cannot keep. I have been in that position myself, and I know the guilt and shame that comes with breaking one's word. However, I also understand the power that a vow can hold over an individual, and how it can shape the course of one's life. In my case, my vanity and pride led me to make promises that I could not keep, and those promises ultimately led to my downfall.

Looking back on my life, I realize that the concept of annulment is not simply about nullifying a vow, but rather about acknowledging the human condition. We are flawed beings, and we make mistakes. We often say things that we do not mean, and we make promises that we cannot keep. However, it is our ability to recognize our faults and seek forgiveness that sets us apart from other creatures. In the end, it is our humanity that defines us, and it is our willingness to admit our shortcomings that makes us truly great.

As I conclude this essay, I am reminded of the words of the great philosopher Friedrich Nietzsche, who once wrote, "All that is necessary for the triumph of evil is that good men do nothing." In the case of annulment, it is not enough to simply nullify a vow and move on. Rather, we must acknowledge the harm that our words can cause, and we must work to make amends for our mistakes. In doing so, we can rise above our human nature and become the best versions of ourselves.

> Dorian Gray is a young, handsome man who becomes corrupted by his own vanity and hedonism. His portrait, which ages and shows the effects of his sins, becomes a haunting reminder of his true nature.

MASEI

Parashat Masei, the concluding portion of the book of Numbers in the Hebrew Bible, is a rich and complex text that invites us to explore the themes of journey, memory, and destiny. And yet, as a writer who has long been fascinated by the power of numbers and their symbolic meanings, I cannot help but be drawn to one particular aspect of this parashah: the number 42.

Now, some of you may be wondering why I am so fixated on this seemingly arbitrary number. To understand my fascination, let me take you on a journey through time and space, to a planet called Earth, where a young man named Arthur Dent found himself caught up in an adventure of cosmic proportions. I am, of course, referring to my novel, The Hitchhiker's Guide to the Galaxy, in which I introduced the concept of the number 42 as the "Answer to the Ultimate Question of Life, the Universe, and Everything."

As many of you know, this idea was born out of a moment of whimsy and frustration, as I struggled to come up with a suitably absurd and yet profound answer to this most fundamental of questions. And so, I turned to my trusty computer, which informed me that the answer was, indeed, 42. Of course, the real challenge was figuring out what the question was in the first place, but that is a story for another time.

What does all of this have to do with Parashat Masei, you ask? Well, as it turns out, the number 42 appears not just in my novel, but also in this portion of the Torah. Specifically, in Numbers 33:1-49, we are presented with a detailed account of the Israelites' travels through the wilderness, listing each of the 42 encampments they made on their journey from Egypt to the Promised Land.

Now, to be clear, I do not believe that the authors of the Torah were consciously referencing my novel when they included this list of 42 encampments. And yet, the fact that this number appears in both contexts is too striking to ignore. It suggests to me that there is something about the number 42 that speaks to our collective unconscious, something that resonates with us on a deep and fundamental level.

So, what might this resonance be? For me, the number 42 represents a kind of cosmic mystery, a tantalizing clue that hints at the existence of a grand design or purpose to the universe. It reminds me that even in the midst of chaos and uncertainty, there is a hidden order that we can glimpse if we look hard enough. And it invites us to ask the big questions, to seek out the meaning and purpose of our existence.

Of course, the answer to those questions may elude us, just as the answer to the Ultimate Question eluded the characters in my novel. But the pursuit of those answers is what gives our lives meaning and purpose. It is what makes us human.

So, as we reflect on Parashat Masei and the number 42, let us embrace the mystery and the wonder of it all. Let us continue to journey through life with curiosity and openness, seeking out the answers to life's big questions even as we revel in the joy and beauty of the journey itself. And let us never forget the power of a good joke, even when it contains the most profound truths of all.

> DOUGLAS ADAMS WAS A BRITISH AUTHOR AND HUMORIST, BEST KNOWN FOR HIS SCIENCE FICTION SERIES "THE HITCHHIKER'S GUIDE TO THE GALAXY". HE WAS ALSO A SCRIPTWRITER AND A PASSIONATE ADVOCATE FOR ENVIRONMENTAL CONSERVATION.

IN THE STYLE OF MOTHER THERESA

My dear brothers and sisters,

As we reflect on Parashat Masei, we are reminded of the importance of compassion and justice in our lives. This week's Torah portion discusses the concept of the Cities of Refuge, where individuals who have unintentionally caused the death of another person can find sanctuary.

As I read this passage, I am reminded of the work that we do every day to help those who have been marginalized and oppressed. We provide a refuge for those who have been cast out by society, who have been forgotten by their communities, and who have been left to suffer alone.

Just as the Cities of Refuge offered a safe haven for those seeking protection from harm, we too must offer a refuge for those who are vulnerable and in need. We must be a beacon of hope and love for those who have been abandoned and left to fend for themselves.

But it is not enough to simply provide a place of refuge. We must also work to address the root causes of suffering and injustice. We must work to create a society that is just and compassionate, where every person is valued and respected.

This is the work that we have dedicated our lives to, and it is a work that we cannot do alone. We must work together, hand in hand, to create a better world for all.

So let us continue to be a light in the darkness, offering hope and love to all who come to us in need. Let us work tirelessly to create a world where everyone has access to the refuge they need to thrive and grow.

May we all be blessed with the strength, courage, and compassion to make this world a better place for all.

With love and peace,

Mother Teresa

MOTHER TERESA, BORN AGNES GONXHA BOJAXHIU, WAS AN ALBANIAN-INDIAN ROMAN CATHOLIC NUN AND MISSIONARY. SHE FOUNDED THE MISSIONARIES OF CHARITY, A CONGREGATION THAT PROVIDES HOSPICE CARE, ORPHANAGES, AND OTHER CHARITABLE SERVICES TO THE POOR.

I am often drawn to stories of journeys, both physical and spiritual. The Torah portion of Parashat Masei is a fascinating account of the Israelites' travels through the wilderness, and as I read it, I am struck by the many parallels between their journey and my own.

The Israelites were a nomadic people, constantly on the move as they followed God's commandments and searched for a homeland. Their journey was not an easy one – they faced many challenges and hardships along the way, from hunger and thirst to attacks from hostile tribes. Despite these difficulties, however, they remained steadfast in their faith and commitment to their mission.

In many ways, this reminds me of my own travels. Like the Israelites, I have often found myself in unfamiliar and sometimes dangerous territory, facing obstacles and adversity at every turn. But just as they did, I have always relied on my faith and my determination to see me through.

One of the most striking aspects of the Israelites' journey is the way in which they marked each stage of their progress. At every stopping place, they erected a pillar of stones to commemorate their journey and to signal the way for future generations. This act of remembrance and celebration was an important part of their journey, helping them to maintain a sense of purpose and direction as they moved ever closer to their goal.

As a writer, I too am acutely aware of the importance of marking each stage of my own journey. Every new place I visit, every new experience I have, is an opportunity to reflect on where I have been and where I am going. I record my thoughts and observations in my journals, and use these reflections to inform my writing and to guide my future travels.

Ultimately, the Israelites' journey was not just a physical one – it was also a spiritual journey. Through their trials and tribulations, they learned important lessons about themselves and about God. They were transformed by their experiences, and emerged from their journey as a stronger, more resilient people.

I too have been transformed by my travels. Each new place I visit, each new person I meet, opens up new horizons and new possibilities for growth and learning. And just as the Israelites found their way to the Promised Land, so too do I find my way to new insights and new experiences.

In conclusion, the story of the Israelites' journey through the wilderness is a powerful reminder of the transformative power of travel. Whether we are journeying through the physical world or through our own spiritual landscape, we are always growing and changing, becoming more fully ourselves. As we travel, we leave behind us a trail of stones, marking our progress and reminding us of the wonders we have seen and the lessons we have learned. And in the end, it is this journey – this lifelong pilgrimage – that defines us and gives our lives meaning.

FREYA STARK (1893-1993) WAS A BRITISH EXPLORER AND TRAVEL WRITER KNOWN FOR HER ADVENTUROUS SPIRIT AND VIVID STORYTELLING. SHE TRAVELED EXTENSIVELY THROUGHOUT THE MIDDLE EAST, PRODUCING NUMEROUS BOOKS ON HER EXPERIENCES.

DEUTERONOMY/DEVARIM

Deuteronomy, Memory, and Legacy

IN THE STYLE OF RABBI MENACHEM CREDITOR

The Book of Deuteronomy is a powerful testament to the enduring nature of memory and legacy. This final book of the Torah is a poignant reflection on the journey of the Israelites from slavery in Egypt to their eventual settlement in the Promised Land. Throughout the book, we see a constant emphasis on the importance of remembering one's past, of carrying the lessons of one's ancestors forward, and of building a legacy that will endure for generations to come.

At the heart of this emphasis on memory and legacy is the idea that we are not just individuals living in isolation, but rather members of a community with a shared history and destiny. The Book of Deuteronomy stresses that the people of Israel are part of a larger story that began with Abraham and Sarah and continues to this day. We are called to remember the trials and triumphs of our ancestors and to draw strength and inspiration from their example.

One of the most powerful passages in Deuteronomy is the Shema, which is recited by Jews every day as a declaration of faith. The Shema begins with the words "Hear, O Israel: the Lord our God, the Lord is one." This simple statement of monotheism is followed by a call to love God with all one's heart, soul, and might. But the Shema goes beyond just affirming our belief in God. It also reminds us of our duty to pass on our faith to the next generation: "And these words that I command you today shall be on your heart. You shall teach them diligently to your children, and shall talk of them when you sit in your house, and when you walk by the way, and when you lie down, and when you rise."

This call to teach our children is a powerful reminder of the importance of memory and legacy. We are not just called to remember our past; we are called to actively transmit it to the next generation. This is the only way to ensure that our story continues to be told and that our legacy endures.

But memory and legacy are not just about the past. They are also about the present and the future. The Book of Deuteronomy calls on us to remember not just what has come before, but also what is happening now and what is yet to come. We are called to be mindful of the needs of those around us and to work to create a just and compassionate society.

In many ways, the Book of Deuteronomy is a call to action. It reminds us that we are not just passive recipients of a legacy; we are active participants in its creation. We are called to build a world that reflects the values and teachings of our ancestors, and to work to ensure that those values and teachings continue to shape the future.

This idea of memory as an active force is at the heart of the Book of Deuteronomy. We are not just called to remember our past; we are called to actively engage with it, to make it part of our present and our future. Through our actions, we can ensure that our legacy endures and that our story continues to be told for generations to come.

DEVARIM

Parashat Devarim, the opening portion of the book of Deuteronomy, contains some of the most profound and timeless themes in the entire Hebrew Bible. At its core, Devarim is a retelling of the story of the Israelites' journey from Egypt to the Promised Land, with a particular focus on Moses' role as leader and teacher. This theme of the telling and retelling of stories is one that is familiar to science fiction fans, as it is a central motif in my work.

In my Foundation series, I show how the telling and retelling of stories can shape the destiny of entire civilizations. In the first book, "Foundation," we are introduced to the idea of psychohistory, a science that can predict the future behavior of large groups of people based on their past actions. The protagonist of the book, Hari Seldon, is a psychohistorian who predicts the collapse of the Galactic Empire and the ensuing chaos that will ensue.

But Seldon doesn't just predict the future; he takes steps to shape it. He establishes a foundation on the edge of the galaxy, where he and his disciples will work to preserve the knowledge of civilization and build a new society that can survive the coming dark age. In order to do this, Seldon relies on the power of storytelling. He creates a series of "Encyclopedists" who are tasked with recording and preserving the knowledge of the past. He also creates a religion, based on the idea of the "Seldon Plan," which gives people a sense of purpose and direction.

In many ways, the story of Moses in Devarim is a similar tale. Moses is a leader who has seen the future and knows what needs to be done to shape it. He knows that the Israelites must remember their past, their journey from slavery to freedom, in order to understand their present and create a better future. And so, he retells the story of the Israelites' journey, reminding them of their past mistakes and victories, and urging them to follow God's commandments.

But Moses is not just a storyteller; he is also a teacher. He doesn't just retell the story of the Israelites' journey; he explains its meaning and relevance for the present. He teaches the Israelites about the importance of justice, mercy, and compassion, and he warns them against the dangers of idolatry and disobedience.

The power of storytelling is evident throughout Devarim. Moses uses stories to educate, inspire, and warn his people. He tells the story of the spies who were sent to scout out the Promised Land, and how their fear and lack of faith led to forty years of wandering in the wilderness. He tells the story of the defeat of Og, king of Bashan, and how God gave the Israelites the strength to overcome their enemies. And he tells the story of the giving of the Ten Commandments, and how these laws are the foundation of a just and moral society.

Storytelling and the retelling of stories are central to both Parashat Devarim and my writing. Both Moses and Hari Seldon understand the power of stories to shape the destiny of individuals and civilizations. They use storytelling to educate, inspire, and warn their people, and to create a sense of purpose and direction. Ultimately, both Devarim and the Foundation series remind us of the importance of remembering our past, learning from our mistakes, and working to create a better future.

> Isaac Asimov was an American writer and professor of biochemistry known for his influential works of science fiction and popular science.

I am fascinated by stories of mythical journeys and the themes of personal transformation that often accompany them. In Parashat Devarim, we see the story of Moses, who embarks on a journey of self-discovery and growth that transforms him from a hesitant and uncertain leader to a confident and powerful figure who is able to guide his people through the wilderness and towards their destiny.

The story of Moses is one of the most powerful and enduring stories in the Hebrew Bible, and it speaks to us on a deep and profound level about the human experience. Like Moses, we are all on a journey of self-discovery and growth, and we must confront the challenges and obstacles that come our way with courage and determination.

The journey of Moses is also a story of the power of faith and the importance of trust in a higher power. As he leads his people through the wilderness, Moses must constantly rely on his faith in God to guide him and to give him the strength and wisdom he needs to overcome the obstacles that he faces.

For me, as a writer and a person, the story of Moses is a powerful reminder of the importance of faith, courage, and determination in the face of adversity. It speaks to the deep human longing for meaning and purpose in life, and it reminds us that we are all on a journey of self-discovery and growth that requires us to confront our fears and our doubts with faith and courage.

At the same time, the story of Moses also speaks to the power of mythic journeys as a literary and spiritual device. The journey of Moses is a classic example of the hero's journey, which is a common theme in many myths and legends from around the world.

The hero's journey is a pattern of narrative that involves a protagonist who embarks on a journey of self-discovery and growth, faces challenges and obstacles, and ultimately emerges transformed and empowered. This pattern of narrative is found in many cultures and traditions, and it speaks to the deep human need for stories that help us to make sense of our lives and our experiences.

As a writer, I am fascinated by the power of mythic journeys to inspire and transform us. In my own writing, I have often explored themes of personal transformation and growth, and I have used the hero's journey as a template for many of my stories.

For me, the hero's journey is a powerful metaphor for the human experience, and it reminds us that we are all on a journey of self-discovery and growth that requires us to face our fears and our doubts with courage and determination. Like Moses, we must trust in a higher power to guide us and to give us the strength and wisdom we need to overcome the challenges and obstacles that we face along the way.

In conclusion, the story of Moses in Parashat Devarim is a powerful example of the themes of personal transformation and mythic journeys that have inspired writers and readers for centuries. I am particularly drawn to these themes, and I believe that they speak to the deep human longing for meaning and purpose in life. Through the story of Moses, we are reminded of the power of faith, courage, and determination to help us overcome the challenges and obstacles that we face on our own journeys of self-discovery and growth.

> Emily Brontë was a 19th-century English novelist and poet, best known for her only novel "Wuthering Heights."

IN THE STYLE OF JOHN ADAMS

Parashat Devarim is an important portion of the Torah that narrates the events that occurred before the Israelites' entry into the Promised Land. It is a powerful story of courage, leadership, and faith that resonates with me as I reflect on my own experiences in political life.

Parashat Devarim recounts Moses' final speech to the Israelites before he passes on the leadership to Joshua. In this speech, Moses reminds the people of their history and their covenant with God, and he implores them to be faithful and courageous as they prepare to enter the Promised Land. Moses, despite his age and physical limitations, embodies personal courage in this moment, showing his determination to fulfill God's plan and lead his people to their destiny.

As I reflect on my own political career, I am struck by the importance of personal courage in leadership. In my role as a Founding Father of the United States and as its second president, I faced numerous challenges and obstacles, including the Revolutionary War, the formation of a new government, and the pressures of international diplomacy. At every turn, I was called upon to display personal courage, to stand up for what I believed in, and to lead by example.

One of the most significant moments of personal courage in my career came during the presidency of my successor, Thomas Jefferson. In 1801, Jefferson defeated me in a bitterly contested election, and I faced the difficult task of transferring power to a political rival who I believed would endanger the very principles of our young democracy. Despite my misgivings, I recognized that the peaceful transfer of power was essential to the stability of our government and the success of our nation. I put aside my personal feelings and worked to ensure a smooth transition, setting a precedent that has endured to this day.

The issue of succession is a critical one in any political system, and it is one that is addressed in Parashat Devarim. Moses passes on the mantle of leadership to Joshua, ensuring that the Israelites have a strong and capable leader to guide them into the Promised Land. Similarly, in the United States, the peaceful transfer of power from one president to another is a cornerstone of our democratic system. It is a testament to the strength of our institutions and the resilience of our democracy that we have been able to maintain this tradition for more than two centuries.

In conclusion, Parashat Devarim is a powerful reminder of the importance of personal courage in leadership. As I reflect on my own experiences in political life, I am struck by the similarities between the challenges faced by Moses and the Israelites and those faced by me and my fellow Founding Fathers. We too were called upon to display personal courage, to stand up for what we believed in, and to lead by example. And like Moses, we recognized the importance of succession, of passing on the mantle of leadership to ensure the continuity of our institutions and the success of our nation.

John Adams was an American statesman, attorney, diplomat, and Founding Father who served as the second President of the United States.

VA'ETCHANAN

IN THE STYLE OF LEAH

As I reflect on Parashat Va'etchanan and the concept of failure, I cannot help but feel a deep sense of resonance with the story of Moses and his struggle to enter the Promised Land. As Leah, one of the matriarchs of the Jewish people, I am all too familiar with the pain of disappointment and the will to thrive against all odds.

My story is one of perseverance in the face of adversity. I was initially seen as the less desirable wife of Jacob, who was in love with my sister Rachel. Despite this, I remained steadfast in my faith and commitment to her family. In the end, I was rewarded with six sons and a daughter, becoming the mother of half of the tribes of Israel.

One legend suggests that my eyes were weak, and that I cried every day because of her unhappy marriage to Jacob. It was only when I prayed to God and asked for a child that my eyes were healed. Another midrash suggests that I was so committed to her family that I agreed to switch places with Rachel on her wedding night to prevent my sister from feeling embarrassed.

Despite these challenges, I continued to thrive and persevere. I knew that my role in the family was essential, and I refused to let my disappointment or sadness define me. Instead, I focused on the things I could control, such as my faith and my dedication to her children.

In many ways, my challenges mirror those faced by Moses in Parashat Va'etchanan. Like me, Moses had a deep commitment to his people and a strong desire to lead them to the Promised Land. However, despite his best efforts, he was ultimately unable to enter it.

This failure was undoubtedly painful for Moses, but it did not define him. He continued to lead his people with courage and determination, knowing that his role was still essential to their survival. In the end, Moses' legacy lived on, inspiring generations of Jewish leaders to come.

Stories like mine and Moses' remind us of the importance of perseverance in the face of adversity. Failure is a part of life, but it does not have to define us. Instead, we can use our challenges as opportunities to grow and thrive, just as Moses and I did.

As we read Parashat Va'etchanan, let us remember that our faith and commitment to our goals can help us overcome even the most significant obstacles. May we all find the strength to persevere in the face of failure and the courage to keep moving forward, no matter what challenges may come our way.

LEAH WAS MOTHER OF SIX OF THE TRIBES OF ISRAEL.

As I reflect upon Parashat Va'etchanan, I cannot help but think about the theme of failure that permeates the narrative. The Torah recounts the story of Moses, who, after leading the Israelites for 40 years, was denied entry into the Promised Land due to his own missteps. As I consider this story, I am reminded of my own experiences with failure, both on and off the screen. I know all too well the feeling of falling short, of not achieving the goals I had set for myself. However, I also know that failure is an integral part of life, and that it is through our mistakes and missteps that we learn and grow.

In the story of Moses, we see a leader who has dedicated his life to his people, leading them out of slavery and through the wilderness. Yet, when he comes to the end of his journey, he is unable to complete it. Despite his pleading with God, he is denied entry into the Promised Land, and is forced to watch as the Israelites continue on without him. This must have been a devastating blow for Moses, who had given so much to his people, only to fall short at the end. Yet, even in this moment of failure, Moses teaches us an important lesson.

In his final address to the Israelites, Moses tells them to remember the commandments that God has given them, and to teach them to their children. He reminds them of the importance of keeping the covenant with God, and of the consequences that come with straying from it. In this way, Moses shows us that even in failure, there is still the opportunity to teach and to lead. While he may not have been able to enter the Promised Land, Moses was still able to impart his wisdom and knowledge to the next generation of Israelites.

I have also experienced failure in my own life. Despite my success on the screen, I have had my fair share of setbacks and disappointments. Yet, it is through these failures that I have been able to learn and grow. In fact, some of my most iconic moments on screen were born out of my own personal struggles. The character of the Tramp, for example, was inspired by my own experiences of poverty and hardship. And in films like City Lights and Modern Times, I explored themes of inequality and social injustice that were close to my heart.

In many ways, the story of Moses and the theme of failure in Parashat Va'etchanan remind us that failure is not something to be feared or avoided. Rather, it is an integral part of life, and one that can lead to growth and learning. Whether we are leaders like Moses, or actors like myself, we must learn to embrace our failures and use them as opportunities to teach and to inspire others. For it is through our failures that we become truly human, and it is through our struggles that we find the strength to overcome.

> CHARLIE CHAPLIN WAS A COMEDIC ACTOR, FILMMAKER, AND COMPOSER WHO ROSE TO FAME IN THE SILENT FILM ERA AND BECAME ONE OF THE MOST ICONIC FIGURES IN THE HISTORY OF CINEMA.

IN THE STYLE OF LUKE SKYWALKER

As I delve into the words of Parashat Va'etchanan, I am reminded of the journey my friends and I took to bring freedom to the galaxy. It was a long and arduous journey, filled with unknown places and unexpected twists, but we remained steadfast in our mission to defeat the dark forces that threatened to engulf us.

The parashah begins with Moses recounting his pleas to God to be allowed to enter the Promised Land. Though he is denied this request, he continues to guide the Israelites, teaching them the laws and commandments that will sustain them as a nation. Similarly, my own journey to freedom began with a plea to my mentor, Obi-Wan Kenobi, to train me in the ways of the Jedi. Despite his initial reluctance, he saw potential in me and took me under his wing.

Our journey took us to many unknown places, each with its own challenges and lessons. One such place was the planet Dagobah, where I sought the guidance of the wise Jedi master, Yoda. Here, I learned the importance of humility and patience, as Yoda taught me to let go of my fear and embrace the Force.

Similarly, the Israelites faced many challenges on their journey to freedom, including battles with hostile nations and the threat of starvation and dehydration in the wilderness. Through it all, they were sustained by their faith in God and their commitment to each other as a community.

As we continued our journey, we encountered unexpected allies and foes alike. One such ally was Lando Calrissian, who helped us infiltrate the Empire's stronghold on the planet of Endor. However, we also faced treachery from within our own ranks, as my own father, Darth Vader, sought to turn me to the dark side.

Similarly, the Israelites faced challenges from within their own community, as some members rebelled against Moses' leadership and sought to worship idols. However, through it all, they remained committed to their collective goal of reaching the Promised Land and establishing a just society.

Ultimately, both our journeys culminated in a great battle against the forces of darkness. For the Israelites, this battle took place as they conquered the Canaanite nations and established their own kingdom. For us, it was the final confrontation with the Empire, culminating in the destruction of the Death Star and the downfall of the Sith.

In both cases, these battles were not just physical, but also symbolic of a deeper struggle for freedom and justice. They represented the triumph of the human spirit over oppression and tyranny, and the power of collective action to achieve a shared goal.

As I reflect on these stories, I am reminded of the importance of community and collective action in the face of adversity. Just as the Israelites were sustained by their faith in God and their commitment to each other, we too were sustained by our faith in the Force and our belief in the power of unity and solidarity.

In conclusion, Parashat Va'etchanan and my own journey to freedom both remind us that the path to liberation is never easy, and that it requires us to confront our fears and work together to overcome the challenges that lie ahead. By embracing the unknown and remaining committed to our shared goals, we can transform ourselves and our communities, and build a better world for all.

> Luke Skywalker is a heroic Jedi Knight who played a pivotal role in the Galactic Civil War and helped bring balance to the Force.

EIKEV

In the Style of Simon Wiesenthal

Parashat Ekev is an important part of the Book of Deuteronomy, containing several significant themes that remain relevant even today. As a survivor of the Holocaust and a renowned Nazi hunter, I am acutely aware of the importance of forgiveness and its role in shaping the future.

One of the most powerful messages of this portion is the idea that forgiveness is an essential part of the human experience. In Deuteronomy 10:17-19, we are reminded that God loves the stranger, and that we should love them too.

In my book "The Sunflower," I grapple with the question of forgiveness in the aftermath of the Holocaust. As a young man, I was approached by a dying SS soldier who asked for his forgiveness for his crimes against Jews. I struggled with what to do in this situation, and ultimately chose not to forgive the soldier. The book explores the complex ethical and moral questions surrounding forgiveness, and ultimately leaves the reader with the idea that forgiveness is a deeply personal decision that cannot be made lightly.

As I reflect on Parashat Ekev, I am struck by the fact that forgiveness is not an easy or simple concept. It is not something that can be demanded or expected, but rather must be earned through genuine remorse and a commitment to making amends. In the case of the SS soldier, Wiesenthal was unable to forgive because the soldier did not demonstrate any true remorse for his actions. In other situations, forgiveness may be possible if the wrongdoer is willing to make amends and take responsibility for their actions.

Another important lesson from both Parashat Ekev is the idea that forgiveness does not mean forgetting or excusing wrongdoing. We must hold people accountable for their actions, and seek justice when necessary. Forgiveness does not mean that we condone or ignore injustice, but rather that we choose to let go of our anger and resentment towards the person who wronged us.

In conclusion, Parashat Ekev provides important insights into the concept of forgiveness. As a survivor of the Holocaust, I have thought deeply about the role of forgiveness in my own life, and have come to believe that it is a deeply personal decision that cannot be made lightly. Forgiveness must be earned through genuine remorse and a commitment to making amends, and does not mean forgetting or excusing wrongdoing. Ultimately, forgiveness is a choice that each of us must make for ourselves, and it is up to us to decide whether we are ready to let go of our anger and resentment towards those who have wronged us.

Simon Wiesenthal was a Holocaust survivor and Nazi hunter who dedicated his life to bringing Nazi war criminals to justice.

IN THE STYLE OF LENA RICHARD

As I reflect on Parashat Eikev, I can't help but think about the "land of milk and honey" and the abundance of the seven grains of the Land of Israel. These agricultural gifts from God represent the nourishment and sustenance that the land provides to the Jewish community.

Food has always played a crucial role in shaping community and cultural identity, and the black food culture is a prime example of this. As a chef and culinary historian, I have seen firsthand how food can bring people together, create shared experiences and memories, and even preserve traditions.

In the black community, food has always been a source of strength and resilience. Despite facing centuries of oppression and hardship, black Americans have used food as a way to connect with their roots, celebrate their heritage, and build community.

From soul food to West African cuisine, the flavors and techniques of black cooking have been passed down from generation to generation, serving as a reminder of the resilience and creativity of the black community.

Just like the seven grains of the Land of Israel, these culinary traditions have become a source of pride and identity for black Americans. They have provided sustenance during times of struggle and joy during times of celebration.

As I prepare meals in my kitchen, I am constantly reminded of the power of food to bring people together. Whether it's a shared family meal or a community event, food has the ability to create connections and strengthen relationships.

> LENA RICHARD WAS A PIONEERING AFRICAN-AMERICAN CHEF, COOKBOOK AUTHOR, AND TELEVISION PERSONALITY WHO CHAMPIONED CREOLE CUISINE AND HELPED PRESERVE ITS LEGACY FOR FUTURE GENERATIONS.

Parashat Eikev is a chapter in the book of Deuteronomy that is filled with warnings and exhortations from Moses to the Israelites. In it, he warns them not to forget God's commandments and to always remember the blessings that God has bestowed upon them. He also warns them not to become complacent and to remember their humble origins as slaves in Egypt.

However, one of the most striking features of this chapter is its emphasis on intergroup violence. Moses warns the Israelites that when they enter the land of Canaan, they will encounter nations that are stronger and more numerous than they are. He tells them that these nations will be destroyed by God, but that the Israelites must also take up arms against them.

This emphasis on violence is troubling, especially given the violence that has characterized so much of human history. It is easy to see how the Israelites, in their desire to secure their own safety and prosperity, could become caught up in a cycle of violence that would only lead to further bloodshed and suffering.

But there is another side to this story. Throughout the Torah, there is a consistent theme of peacemaking and reconciliation. God commands the Israelites to love their neighbors as themselves, to treat the stranger with kindness and respect, and to seek justice and righteousness in all their dealings.

In Parashat Eikev, Moses reminds the Israelites of this commandment, telling them that they must not only defeat their enemies, but also show them kindness and compassion. He tells them that they must not oppress the widow or the orphan, and that they must remember their own experiences of slavery and oppression.

This emphasis on compassion and kindness is a crucial reminder of the importance of peacemaking. In a world where violence and conflict seem all too common, it is easy to forget that there is another way. We can choose to be compassionate, to seek understanding and reconciliation, and to work for peace.

This is not to say that there are not times when violence is necessary. The Israelites, in their struggle to secure their own safety and survival, had little choice but to take up arms against their enemies. But even in the midst of war and conflict, there is always room for compassion and kindness.

The message of Parashat Eikev is a powerful reminder of this truth. It calls on us to remember our common humanity, to treat others with respect and kindness, and to work for peace and reconciliation whenever possible. It reminds us that even in the midst of conflict and violence, there is always a better way – a way of compassion and understanding that can lead to healing and reconciliation.

> Howard Zinn was an American historian, playwright, and social activist best known for his book "A People's History of the United States," which presents American history from the perspective of the oppressed and marginalized.

RE'EH

My dear friends, as I sit here and ponder the words of Parashat Re'eh, I am struck by the theme of freedom that is woven throughout its verses. It is a theme that resonates deeply with me, as I myself have struggled for freedom throughout my life.

In this parashah, we see the importance of choice and the consequences that come with it. The Torah says, "I have set before you life and death, blessing and curse. Choose life so that you and your descendants may live" (Deuteronomy 30:19). This powerful statement reminds us that we have the power to choose our own path in life, but we must also bear the responsibility for our choices.

For me, the quest for freedom was not simply a matter of choice. As a black woman in America, I was born into slavery and had no say in my own fate. But I refused to accept my bondage as my destiny. I fought for my freedom, and I spoke out against the injustice of slavery.

Parashat Re'eh speaks to the power of our words and actions. We are called to be responsible for the impact we have on others and the world around us. The Torah says, "Take heed and listen to these words that I command you, so that it may go well with you and with your children after you forever" (Deuteronomy 12:28). We must use our words and actions to create a better world for ourselves and for future generations.

For me, this meant using my voice to advocate for freedom and justice. I traveled across the country, giving speeches and sharing my story with others. I believed that by speaking out, I could inspire others to join the fight for freedom.

Parashat Re'eh also reminds us of the importance of community. The Torah says, "See, I am setting before you today a blessing and a curse: the blessing, if you obey the commandments of the Lord your God that I am commanding you today; and the curse, if you do not obey the commandments of the Lord your God" (Deuteronomy 11:26-28). We are all responsible for each other, and we must work together to create a better world.

As I fought for my own freedom, I also worked to create a community of like-minded individuals who shared my passion for justice. Together, we fought for the abolition of slavery and for women's rights. We recognized that we were stronger together than we could ever be alone.

In conclusion, Parashat Re'eh speaks to the universal human desire for freedom. We all have the power to choose our own path in life and to make a difference in the world around us. But we must also remember that we are responsible for our words and actions, and we must work together to create a better world for ourselves and future generations. May we all be inspired by the words of this parashah and work towards a world where freedom and justice reign.

> Sojourner Truth was an African American abolitionist and women's rights activist who delivered the famous "Ain't I a Woman?" speech in 1851.

IN THE STYLE OF VINCENT VAN GOGH

As I contemplate the words of Parashat Re'eh, I am struck by the idea that "seeing is believing." This phrase has always resonated with me, as an artist who relies on my visual senses to create my art. But what does it mean to truly believe what you see? As I delve deeper into the text, I am reminded of the power of perception and the importance of looking beyond the surface.

As a painter, I am constantly trying to capture the essence of what I see before me. I strive to bring my own perspective to life on the canvas, to create something that is both beautiful and meaningful. But as I study the words of Parashat Re'eh, I am reminded that there is more to seeing than just the act of looking. We must also be willing to truly see what is before us, to open ourselves up to the possibility of new perspectives and deeper truths.

In the parashah, we are told to "see" the blessings and curses that come with our choices. We are reminded that our actions have consequences, and that we must choose wisely if we want to reap the rewards of a righteous life. But what does it mean to truly "see" these blessings and curses? It is not enough to simply acknowledge their existence; we must also understand their significance and take responsibility for our choices.

For me, this idea of truly seeing the world around us is what makes art so powerful. As an artist, I strive to create works that inspire others to see the world in a new way. I want to challenge my viewers to look beyond the surface, to see the beauty and complexity of the world around us. But in order to do this, we must be willing to see things as they truly are, rather than just as we want them to be.

As I paint, I am constantly reminded of the importance of perception. The same object can look completely different depending on the angle from which it is viewed. It is up to us as artists (and as people) to open ourselves up to new perspectives and to see things as they truly are. This is not always an easy task, but it is one that is necessary if we want to live a life of meaning and purpose.

> VINCENT VAN GOGH WAS A DUTCH POST-IMPRESSIONIST PAINTER WHO IS WIDELY RECOGNIZED AS ONE OF THE GREATEST AND MOST INFLUENTIAL ARTISTS OF ALL TIME.

In Parashat Re'eh, found in the book of Deuteronomy in the Hebrew Bible, there is a powerful statement: "You shall not add to the word that I command you, nor shall you subtract from it, to observe the commandments of the Lord your God that I command you" (Deuteronomy 4:2). This phrase is often interpreted as a warning against altering the laws and commandments given to the Israelites by God. It speaks to the importance of preserving the integrity of the law and recognizing its role as a fundamental aspect of society. In this essay, I will explore the implications of this phrase and its relevance to the concept of common law and law as a living tradition.

A strong, centralized government is necessary for a stable society. Without this authority, people would naturally fall into a state of chaos and war. The law is the foundation of this authority, and that it is necessary to maintain the law in order to maintain order. The law is not a static entity, but rather a living tradition that evolved over time. This evolution is essential to the success of the law, as it allowed it to adapt to changing circumstances and address new challenges.

Similarly, the phrase "Do not add or subtract from these commandments" suggests that the law is not fixed, but rather a dynamic entity that evolves over time. It acknowledges that the law must adapt to changing circumstances, while also recognizing the importance of preserving its core principles. In this sense, the phrase emphasizes the need to strike a balance between stability and adaptability in the law.

The concept of common law also reflects this balance. Common law is a legal system that is based on precedent and the decisions of judges. It is a living tradition that evolves over time, adapting to changing circumstances and addressing new challenges. At the same time, common law is based on a set of core principles that have been established over centuries of legal practice. These principles provide stability and consistency in the law, while also allowing it to evolve.

The phrase "Do not add or subtract from these commandments" can be seen as a warning against altering the core principles of the law. It recognizes the importance of preserving these principles, while also allowing for adaptation and evolution. Similarly, common law is based on a set of core principles that provide stability and consistency, while also allowing for adaptation and evolution.

In conclusion, the phrase "Do not add or subtract from these commandments" speaks to the importance of preserving the integrity of the law while recognizing its role as a living tradition that evolves over time. This balance between stability and adaptability is essential for a successful legal system. The concept of common law reflects this balance, providing a stable foundation for the law while allowing it to adapt to changing circumstances. Ultimately, both the phrase and the concept of common law emphasize the importance of striking a balance between stability and adaptability in the law.

> THOMAS HOBBES (1588-1679) WAS AN ENGLISH PHILOSOPHER AND POLITICAL THEORIST KNOWN FOR HIS BELIEF IN ABSOLUTE SOVEREIGNTY AND SOCIAL CONTRACT THEORY.

SHOFTIM

Parashat Shoftim speaks to the power of law and its ability to achieve justice. As a lawyer and advocate for civil rights, I have long been inspired by the wisdom contained in this text, and I believe that its teachings are just as relevant today as they were thousands of years ago.

At its core, Parashat Shoftim emphasizes the importance of a just legal system. The portion begins by outlining the need for judges and officers who will "judge the people with righteous judgment" (Deuteronomy 16:18). This emphasis on justice is not just a matter of ensuring that individuals are punished for their wrongdoing; rather, it is about creating a society that is fundamentally fair and just.

Indeed, the Torah makes it clear that justice is not just a matter of punishing the guilty, but also of protecting the vulnerable. The text instructs us to show special concern for the needs of widows, orphans, and strangers – those who are often the most vulnerable members of society (Deuteronomy 16:11, 16:14). This is a powerful reminder that the law is not just about upholding order; it is also about ensuring that the needs of all members of society are met.

But perhaps the most powerful message of Parashat Shoftim is the idea that the law itself has the power to create a just society. The text emphasizes that "justice, justice shall you pursue" (Deuteronomy 16:20) – a phrase that has become a rallying cry for those who seek to create a more just world. This passage reminds us that justice is not something that can be passively awaited; it is something that must be actively pursued.

This pursuit of justice, however, cannot be achieved without a strong legal system. The Torah emphasizes the importance of judges who are "not to show partiality, nor take a bribe" (Deuteronomy 16:19). This is a powerful reminder that the law is not just about upholding the interests of the powerful; it is also about creating a system that is fair and impartial.

As someone who has dedicated my life to the pursuit of justice, I have long been inspired by the teachings of Parashat Shoftim. To me, this text speaks to the fundamental importance of a just legal system – one that is committed to upholding the needs of all members of society, and to ensuring that justice is actively pursued.

But achieving this kind of legal system is not easy. It requires not just the commitment of individuals, but also the strength of institutions. It requires the creation of a legal system that is strong, fair, and impartial – one that is capable of upholding the needs of the most vulnerable members of society, and that is committed to the pursuit of justice.

Ultimately, I believe that the teachings of Parashat Shoftim can serve as a powerful reminder of the importance of the law in achieving justice. This portion reminds us that the law has the power to create a more just society – but only if we are willing to actively pursue justice and commit ourselves to the creation of a legal system that is fundamentally fair and impartial.

> Thurgood Marshall was an American lawyer and civil rights activist who became the first African American to serve on the US Supreme Court.

As an avid reader and scholar of history, I have always been fascinated by the concept of kingship and the power dynamics that come with it. So it comes as no surprise that I was drawn to Parashat Shoftim, which discusses the role and responsibilities of kings in ancient Israel.

The parasha includes the statement: "You shall surely set a king over you, whom the Lord your God shall choose" (Deuteronomy 17:15). This passage sets the stage for the discussion of the king's role and the criteria for selecting him. The text goes on to outline the requirements for a king, emphasizing that he must not acquire excessive wealth or wives, nor should he turn his heart away from God's commandments.

What is striking about this passage is the emphasis on the king's moral character. The Torah sets a high standard for the king, requiring him to be humble, compassionate, and just. In other words, the king is not only a political leader but also a moral one, responsible for ensuring that his kingdom is governed with righteousness and equity.

But the parasha also recognizes the potential dangers of kingship. The text warns that a king who becomes too powerful may become corrupt and abusive, leading the people astray. To prevent this, the Torah imposes certain limitations on the king's power, such as requiring him to consult with the priests and judges and follow their guidance.

This tension between the king's power and his moral responsibilities is something that resonates with me deeply. As someone who has seen the consequences of unchecked power firsthand, I understand the importance of having leaders who are guided by a sense of duty and responsibility to their people.

The role of the king in ancient Israel is also a reminder that leadership is not just about holding power but also about using it for the greater good. The king is not an autocrat but a servant of the people, entrusted with their well-being and prosperity. His success is measured not by his personal achievements but by the welfare of his subjects.

As I reflect on Parashat Shoftim and the lessons it holds for us today, I cannot help but think of the many leaders throughout history who have failed to live up to the standard set by the Torah. Too often, we have seen leaders who are more concerned with their own power and prestige than with the well-being of their people. These leaders have left a trail of devastation in their wake, causing untold suffering and harm.

But I also take heart in the examples of leaders who have risen to the challenge, who have used their power for good and made a positive impact on their societies. These leaders remind us that kingship is not just a title or a position but a calling, a responsibility that requires courage, wisdom, and compassion.

In conclusion, Parashat Shoftim provides us with a powerful reminder of the importance of moral leadership and the responsibilities that come with holding power. The text reminds us that kingship is not just a matter of politics but also of morality, requiring leaders who are guided by a sense of duty to their people and a commitment to justice and righteousness. May we all be inspired by this parasha to seek out leaders who embody these values and strive to make a positive difference in the world.

> TYRION LANNISTER IS A WITTY AND INTELLIGENT MEMBER OF HOUSE LANNISTER, KNOWN FOR HIS SHARP TONGUE AND STRATEGIC MIND IN THE FICTIONAL WORLD OF A SONG OF ICE AND FIRE.

IN THE STYLE OF QUEEN ELIZABETH II

My dear subjects,

Today, I would like to reflect upon Parashat Shoftim, a portion of the Torah that speaks about the appointment of judges and the importance of justice in our society. As someone who has dedicated her life to serving her country and upholding the principles of justice and fairness, this parashah resonates deeply with me.

But as I reflect on Parashat Shoftim, I cannot help but think about the evolving notion of royalty throughout history. When I was born in 1926, the concept of royalty was very different from what it is today. Back then, being a member of the royal family meant living a life of luxury and privilege, with little accountability to the public. But as the world changed, so did our roles as royals.

Today, being a member of the royal family means being held to a higher standard of conduct, and serving the people of our nation with humility and dedication. It means using our platform to promote important causes, and advocating for justice and equality for all.

This evolution of the concept of royalty is reflected in the words of Parashat Shoftim. The portion emphasizes the importance of appointing judges who are just and fair, and who are not swayed by personal biases or corruption. It stresses the need for impartiality and accountability in our justice system, and reminds us that justice is essential to the functioning of society.

As a member of the royal family, I have always taken these principles to heart. Throughout my reign, I have sought to embody the values of justice, fairness, and compassion. I have worked to promote important causes such as education, healthcare, and the environment, and I have strived to build bridges between different communities and nations.

Of course, the role of royalty is not without its challenges. We are often scrutinized by the public and held to a higher standard of conduct than others. But this is a responsibility that we willingly accept, because we believe that our position can be used to do good in the world.

As I look back on my long reign, I am proud of the ways in which the notion of royalty has evolved. We have become more accountable, more humble, and more focused on serving the public. And as we move forward into the future, I am confident that this evolution will continue, as we strive to build a more just and equitable world for all.

May the principles of justice and fairness continue to guide us all, and may we never forget the importance of serving our communities with humility and dedication.

Yours faithfully,
Elizabeth R.

> Elizabeth II was Queen of the United Kingdom and other Commonwealth realms from 6 February 1952 until her death in 2022.

KI TEITZEI

As I read through Parashat Ki Teitzei, I am struck by the vivid and often brutal descriptions of war and its aftermath. This parsha is filled with commandments and laws that are meant to guide us in times of conflict and to help us navigate the ravages of war.

In particular, one passage stands out to me: "When you go out to war against your enemies, and the Lord your God gives them into your hand, and you take them captive, and you see among the captives a beautiful woman, and you desire to take her to be your wife..." (Deuteronomy 21:10-11). This passage is unsettling in many ways, as it seems to condone taking women captive and forcing them into marriage. However, when viewed in the context of the time and place in which it was written, it becomes clear that this passage is not an endorsement of war or its brutal consequences, but rather a recognition of the reality of war and an attempt to mitigate its worst effects.

As a soldier and a leader, I have seen firsthand the ravages of war. I have seen the physical and emotional toll that it can take on those who fight in it, as well as on the civilian populations caught in the crossfire. I have seen the devastation that war can wreak on communities and families, and the long-term consequences that can last for generations.

And yet, as difficult as it may be to accept, war is sometimes necessary. When our enemies threaten our security and our way of life, we must be prepared to defend ourselves and our people. We must be willing to fight for what we believe in, even if it means putting ourselves in harm's way.

But at the same time, we must never forget the human cost of war. We must never lose sight of the fact that every life lost in battle is a tragedy, and every act of violence has a ripple effect that can be felt for years to come. We must do everything in our power to minimize the damage that war can cause, and to work towards a world where conflict is resolved peacefully and justly.

This is where the commandments and laws of Parashat Ki Teitzei can be so valuable. They remind us of the importance of compassion and justice, even in the midst of war. They encourage us to treat our enemies with dignity and respect, and to minimize the harm that we cause to innocent bystanders. And they challenge us to think deeply about the consequences of our actions, and to consider the long-term impact that they will have on our world.

As a leader, I have always believed that the ultimate goal of war should be peace. We must fight when necessary, but we must also work tirelessly to create a world where war is no longer necessary. This requires a commitment to diplomacy, to dialogue, and to the hard work of building bridges across divides. It requires us to be courageous and compassionate, to listen deeply to one another, and to seek common ground wherever possible.

In the end, the message of Parashat Ki Teitzei is one of hope. It reminds us that even in the darkest of times, there is always a path forward. It challenges us to confront the realities of war, but also to imagine a better world, a world where peace reigns and justice prevails. And it calls on us to work tirelessly towards that vision, with all the courage, compassion, and determination that we can muster.

> Yitzhak Rabin was an Israeli statesman and general who served as the Prime Minister of Israel and was awarded the Nobel Peace Prize for his role in the Israeli-Palestinian peace process.

IN THE STYLE OF DR. FRANK-N-FURTER

(Verse 1)
I was reading Torah, just the other day
Found a verse that made me stop and say
"No male garment shall be upon a woman
Nor any woman's garment be upon a man"

(Chorus)
Oh, Ki Teitzei, you've got me feeling queer
With these rules that seem so strict and clear
But I'll be who I am, no matter what they say
In my corset and fishnets, I'll slay

(Verse 2)
I don't care what the Torah says
I'll dress how I please, in any way
I'm a transvestite from Transylvania
And I'm not afraid to cross-dress, no matter what ya

(Chorus)
Oh, Ki Teitzei, you've got me feeling queer
With these rules that seem so strict and clear
But I'll be who I am, no matter what they say
In my corset and fishnets, I'll slay

(Bridge)
I'll strut my stuff in high heels and a skirt
No matter what the rabbi says, it won't hurt
My identity is mine, and I'll express it my way
I won't let these ancient rules keep me at bay

(Chorus)
Oh, Ki Teitzei, you've got me feeling queer
With these rules that seem so strict and clear
But I'll be who I am, no matter what they say
In my corset and fishnets, I'll slay.

DR. FRANK-N-FURTER IS A CHARISMATIC AND SEDUCTIVE ALIEN TRANSVESTITE SCIENTIST FROM THE PLANET TRANSSEXUAL IN THE GALAXY OF TRANSYLVANIA, AND THE MAIN CHARACTER OF THE CULT CLASSIC FILM "THE ROCKY HORROR PICTURE SHOW."

In Parashat Ki Teitzei, we encounter a wide range of laws and regulations that cover various aspects of life, from personal conduct to civic responsibility. As we read through these commandments, we cannot help but notice the emphasis placed on creating a just and compassionate society that upholds the rights and dignity of all its members. This emphasis on civic responsibility is particularly evident in the section that deals with the construction of parapets, which serves as a powerful metaphor for the role that we all play in creating safe and just communities.

The Torah commands us to build a parapet or a guard rail around the roof of our homes, so that no one falls off and gets hurt. This seemingly simple commandment has far-reaching implications for our role as responsible citizens. It underscores the idea that we have a duty not only to protect ourselves but also to safeguard the well-being of others in our community. By building a parapet, we are taking an active role in preventing harm and creating a safe environment for everyone.

Moreover, the construction of parapets is not limited to our own homes. The Torah extends this responsibility to cover public spaces as well, emphasizing that we must build guard rails around any structure that poses a risk of harm to others. This includes everything from wells and cisterns to balconies and staircases. The message here is clear: we are all responsible for the safety and well-being of those around us, and we must take active steps to prevent harm and protect the vulnerable.

At a deeper level, the construction of parapets speaks to the importance of creating a just and equitable society. By taking responsibility for the safety of others, we are acknowledging the interconnectedness of our lives and the importance of building strong and caring communities. We are recognizing that our actions have a ripple effect on those around us, and that by working together, we can create a society that upholds the dignity and rights of all its members.

This emphasis on civic responsibility is not limited to the construction of physical structures like parapets. It extends to all aspects of our lives, from our personal conduct to our interactions with others. We are called upon to act with compassion and justice, to be mindful of the impact of our actions on those around us, and to work towards creating a society that is fair, just, and equitable.

In many ways, the construction of parapets is a metaphor for the broader social and political challenges that we face as a society. It highlights the importance of taking active steps to prevent harm, of recognizing our shared responsibility for the well-being of others, and of building strong and caring communities. It reminds us that we are all connected, and that our actions have a powerful impact on the world around us.

As we reflect on the message of Parashat Ki Teitzei and the construction of parapets, we are reminded of the power and responsibility that we all hold as citizens. We are called upon to act with compassion, justice, and responsibility, to work towards creating a society that upholds the dignity and rights of all its members, and to take active steps to prevent harm and protect the vulnerable. In doing so, we can build a world that is safe, just, and compassionate – a world that reflects the values and ideals of our shared humanity.

> JANE JACOBS WAS AN AMERICAN-CANADIAN JOURNALIST, AUTHOR, AND ACTIVIST KNOWN FOR HER INFLUENTIAL WORK IN URBAN PLANNING AND PRESERVATION.

KI TAVO

IN THE STYLE OF RABBI ALAN LEW

Shalom and blessings to all who are joining me today to explore the weekly Torah portion, Parashat Ki Tavo. This portion discusses the ritual of Bikkurim, which is the practice of bringing the first fruits of the land to the Temple in gratitude to God. This practice is a reminder of the abundance of blessings that we have in our lives and the importance of expressing gratitude for those blessings.

In our modern society, it is easy to become consumed with the busyness of life and forget to take a moment to appreciate the simple things that we often take for granted. The practice of Bikkurim is a powerful tool to help us cultivate mindfulness and gratitude in our daily lives.

One of the key components of the Bikkurim ritual is the recitation of a declaration by the farmer, acknowledging the abundance that God has provided and expressing gratitude for those blessings. This declaration serves as a reminder to us that we must actively cultivate an attitude of gratitude and recognize the good that is present in our lives.

In addition to the recitation of the declaration, the Bikkurim ritual involves a physical act of offering the first fruits to God. This act serves as a symbol of our commitment to acknowledging the blessings in our lives and expressing gratitude for them.

The practice of Bikkurim is not just about expressing gratitude for the physical abundance in our lives, but also about recognizing the spiritual abundance that we have been given. We are blessed with the gift of life, the ability to connect with others, and the opportunity to grow and learn.

As we approach the High Holy Days, it is important to remember the practice of Bikkurim and the importance of cultivating mindfulness and gratitude in our daily lives. By acknowledging the blessings in our lives and expressing gratitude for them, we can create a sense of peace and contentment that will guide us throughout the year.

In conclusion, the ritual of Bikkurim serves as a powerful reminder of the importance of cultivating mindfulness and gratitude in our daily lives. By acknowledging the abundance of blessings that we have in our lives, we can cultivate a sense of peace and contentment that will guide us throughout the year. May we all strive to cultivate an attitude of gratitude and appreciation for the abundance in our lives.

> RABBI ALAN LEW WAS A WRITER, MEDITATION TEACHER, AND SPIRITUAL LEADER KNOWN FOR HIS PIONEERING WORK IN BLENDING JEWISH SPIRITUALITY WITH BUDDHIST MEDITATION PRACTICES.

As a survivor of the Hunger Games and a leader in the rebellion against the Capitol, I have seen firsthand the consequences of an oppressive system that values profit over people. And as I read Parashat Ki Tavo, I couldn't help but see parallels between the problems of fast fashion in our world and the warnings of the Israelites in this ancient text.

One phrase that stood out to me was "your clothing and shoes did not wear out" (Deuteronomy 29:5). This is part of a larger passage in which Moses reminds the Israelites of the covenant between them and God. He reminds them of the hardships they have faced and the miracles they have witnessed, and encourages them to remain faithful to God's commands.

But why is the fact that their clothing and shoes did not wear out important? It speaks to a deeper truth about sustainability and the dangers of our consumer culture. In our world, fast fashion has become a massive industry, with companies churning out cheap, trendy clothing at an alarming rate. The result is a culture of disposability, where we buy clothes that we wear only a few times before throwing them away and buying something new.

This culture of disposability has a devastating impact on the environment, as well as on the workers who make our clothes. Fast fashion companies prioritize speed and profit over sustainability and ethical production, leading to massive amounts of waste and exploitation.

But it doesn't have to be this way. Parashat Ki Tavo reminds us that it is possible to create a sustainable, just society. The fact that the Israelites' clothing and shoes did not wear out suggests that they lived in a society where people valued quality over quantity. They repaired and reused their possessions instead of constantly buying new ones.

We can learn from this example and make changes in our own lives to reduce our impact on the environment and support ethical production. We can choose to buy clothing made from sustainable materials, from companies that prioritize ethical production and fair labor practices. We can repair and reuse the clothing we already have instead of constantly buying new things. We can even learn to make our own clothes, like my friend Madge did in District 12.

These may seem like small actions, but they can have a big impact. By valuing quality over quantity, we can reduce waste and create a more sustainable future. And by supporting ethical production and fair labor practices, we can help create a world where everyone's needs are met and no one is exploited.

So let us remember the warnings of Parashat Ki Tavo, and strive to build a world where our clothing and shoes do not wear out because they are made to last, not because we throw them away after a few wears. We can create a world where sustainability, justice, and compassion are the guiding principles, and where the needs of all are valued over the profits of a few.

> KATNISS EVERDEEN IS A SKILLED ARCHER AND RESOURCEFUL SURVIVOR WHO BECOMES A SYMBOL OF REBELLION AGAINST THE OPPRESSIVE CAPITOL IN THE HUNGER GAMES TRILOGY.

As a firm believer in the values of Judaism and the Torah, I am particularly drawn to Parashat Ki Tavo, which speaks to the importance of social welfare and the responsibility that we have towards the less fortunate members of our society.

In this Parashah, we are instructed to bring the first fruits of our labor to the Kohanim in the Temple, as a way of expressing our gratitude to God for the blessings he has bestowed upon us. We are also commanded to give portions to the Levite, the stranger, the orphan, and the widow. This is a powerful statement about the importance of caring for those in need, and it is a message that continues to resonate with me to this day.

As a philanthropist, I have always felt a deep sense of responsibility towards those less fortunate than myself. I believe that it is our duty to use our resources to make a positive impact on the world, and to help those who are in need. This is why the phrase "You shall also give portions to the Levite, the stranger, the orphan, and the widow" is so meaningful to me. It reminds me that we must always be mindful of the needs of others and do what we can to help.

The Levite, the stranger, the orphan, and the widow are all groups that were particularly vulnerable in ancient times. The Levites were responsible for serving in the Temple, but they did not receive an inheritance of land like the other tribes, so they were dependent on the generosity of others for their sustenance. The stranger was someone who had come from another land and did not have the same support networks as a native-born Israelite. The orphan and the widow were both groups who had lost their primary providers and were in need of assistance.

While the specific circumstances of these groups may have changed over time, the underlying message remains the same: we must be mindful of those who are in need and do what we can to help them. This is a core tenet of Judaism, and it is one that has guided my own philanthropic work throughout my life.

In my own time, I have sought to address the needs of the less fortunate through a wide range of initiatives. I have funded hospitals and schools, supported the establishment of agricultural colonies, and worked to alleviate poverty and hunger among the Jewish community in Israel and around the world. My work has always been driven by a desire to fulfill the commandments of the Torah and to make a positive impact on the world.

As we reflect on Parashat Ki Tavo, I encourage all of us to think about how we can apply its message to our own lives. Whether through charitable giving, volunteering, or other forms of service, we all have a role to play in building a more just and compassionate world. As the Torah reminds us, we must always be mindful of the needs of the less fortunate among us, and do what we can to help.

> Moses Montefiore was a British financier and philanthropist who dedicated his life and wealth to social causes and improving the lives of Jewish people around the world.

NITZAVIM

IN THE STYLE OF RABBI JOSHUA

I find great wisdom in the Parashat Nitzavim, which speaks of the covenant between God and the Israelites. In particular, I am drawn to the verse, "It is not in heaven" (Deuteronomy 30:12), which speaks to the accessibility of God's laws and commandments.

This verse has been the subject of much debate among my fellow sages. Some interpret it to mean that once God gave the Torah to Moses on Mount Sinai, it became the sole province of human interpretation and understanding. Others argue that God continues to play a role in the interpretation of his laws.

As for me, I subscribe to the former interpretation. I believe that God's laws were given to humanity to be understood and applied through our own faculties of reason and interpretation. In other words, God has given us the tools to understand his laws, and it is up to us to use them.

This idea is exemplified in the famous rabbinic debate over the oven of Akhnai. A group of sages debated whether an oven made of separate pieces, like the one in question, could be declared pure or impure. The majority ruled that it was impure, but Rabbi Eliezer, who was known for his great learning and piety, argued that it was pure.

When Rabbi Eliezer called upon various heavenly signs to prove his point, the other sages remained unmoved, and I cited the verse "It is not in heaven" as evidence that God's laws are to be interpreted by humans, not divine intervention.

While Rabbi Eliezer's position was ultimately rejected, his example shows the importance of human interpretation in the understanding of God's laws. As sages, we are tasked with using our own intelligence and learning to grapple with the complexities of God's commandments.

In conclusion, the verse "It is not in heaven" reminds us that God's laws are meant to be accessible to all, and that it is up to us as sages to use our faculties of reason and interpretation to understand and apply them. While divine intervention may sometimes be invoked, ultimately it is human understanding that will guide us in our interpretation of God's laws.

> RABBI JOSHUA WAS A PROMINENT JEWISH SAGE AND LEADER DURING THE TALMUDIC ERA, KNOWN FOR HIS SCHOLARSHIP AND EXPERTISE IN HALAKHA (JEWISH LAW).

For those who may not be familiar, Parashat Nitzavim is a section of the Torah that deals with the idea of choice. Specifically, it discusses how we have the ability to choose between good and evil, life and death. It's a powerful message, and one that has been studied by scholars for centuries.

As a moral philosopher, I find this idea particularly intriguing. After all, the question of choice is at the very heart of moral philosophy. We must constantly decide between right and wrong, good and evil, and it's not always an easy decision.

Take, for example, the famous trolley problem. You know the one – a trolley is hurtling down a track, and you have the ability to switch it to a different track, but doing so would cause the death of one person instead of five. What do you do? It's a moral dilemma that has plagued philosophers for decades.

Similarly, in Parashat Nitzavim, we are faced with a choice between life and death. But what does that mean, exactly? Does it mean that we should always choose life over death, no matter what? Or are there situations in which death is the better option?

These are difficult questions, but ones that we must grapple with if we want to lead a moral life. And I, for one, believe that it's better to grapple with them than to ignore them altogether.

Of course, as with all things, there is a humorous side to all of this. I can just imagine someone saying, "Chidi, I'm not a philosopher, I'm just trying to get through the day. Do I really need to worry about the trolley problem?"

To which I would respond, "Well, my dear friend, it's always good to be prepared. You never know when you might be called upon to make a moral decision. And who knows, maybe one day you'll find yourself in a situation where the trolley problem is a real-life dilemma. Better safe than sorry, right?"

In all seriousness, though, I do believe that the dilemmas of moral philosophy are important for all of us to consider. Whether we're facing a decision about the trolley problem or something more mundane, like whether or not to cheat on our taxes, we must be mindful of our choices and the consequences they may have.

And so, I encourage you all to take a page from Parashat Nitzavim and remember that we have the power of choice. It may not always be easy, but it's worth the effort to lead a moral and fulfilling life. Thank you for listening, and may you always choose wisely.

CHIDI ANAGONYE IS A FICTIONAL CHARACTER FROM THE TV SHOW "THE GOOD PLACE", PORTRAYED AS A MORAL PHILOSOPHY PROFESSOR WITH CHRONIC INDECISIVENESS AND ANXIETY.

In the style of Janusz Korczak

I have always emphasized the importance of education and the preciousness of life. Parashat Nitzavim, a portion of the Torah, also underscores the significance of these values.

In this portion, Moses delivers a powerful message to the Israelites before they enter the Promised Land. He reminds them that they are standing before God, and that all members of the community are equal in God's eyes. The passage states that "you are standing today, all of you, before the Lord your God," emphasizing the unity of the Israelites and the importance of their collective responsibility.

For me, this message resonates deeply, especially when it comes to the role of the educator. As a teacher and mentor to young children, I firmly believe that every child deserves the same respect and care, regardless of their background or social status. Each child is a unique and precious individual, and it is our responsibility as educators to help them reach their full potential and become the best versions of themselves.

However, this task is not always easy. In my work as a director of an orphanage in the Warsaw Ghetto during World War II, I saw firsthand the challenges and dangers of being an educator in a time of crisis. I worked tirelessly to provide the children under my care with love, education, and a sense of community, despite the harsh conditions and the constant threat of deportation to the concentration camps.

Tragically, my life was cut short by the Nazis in 1942 when I was deported along with the children to the Treblinka extermination camp. My dedication to the preciousness of life and the role of the educator remained strong until the very end, as I chose to accompany the children on their journey to their deaths rather than abandon them.

Parashat Nitzavim reminds us of the power of unity and collective responsibility, and the importance of education in shaping the lives of young people. As an educator and advocate for children, I devoted my life to these principles, even in the face of unimaginable adversity. I hope that my legacy can inspire others to carry on this vital work, and to never forget the preciousness of every life.

Janusz Korczak was a Polish-Jewish educator, children's author, and pediatrician who died during the Holocaust while refusing to abandon the children in his care.

VAYELECH

IN THE STYLE OF JEANNETTE RANKIN

As the first woman ever elected to the United States Congress, I have always believed that leadership is crucial to our collective future. And nowhere is this more evident than in Parashat Vayelech, where we see Moses preparing to pass the mantle of leadership to Joshua.

In this parashah, Moses knows that his time on earth is coming to an end. He has led the Israelites through the wilderness, but he will not be able to accompany them into the Promised Land. So, he calls Joshua to his side and charges him with the task of leading the people forward.

This passing of the torch is a powerful reminder of the importance of leadership succession. Moses was a great leader, but he knew that he could not do it all himself. He knew that he needed to identify and groom a successor who would be able to carry on his work after he was gone.

This is a lesson that we must take to heart today. As we face unprecedented challenges in our world, from climate change to inequality to political polarization, we need leaders who can rise to the occasion and guide us forward.

And yet, too often, we see a lack of foresight when it comes to leadership succession. Whether it's in business, politics, or other areas of life, we see leaders who cling to power and refuse to think about the future. They may be effective in the short term, but in the long run, they are doing a disservice to their organizations and to society as a whole.

That's why we need to cultivate a new generation of leaders who are committed to building a better future. We need leaders who are willing to think beyond their own self-interest and work towards a common goal. We need leaders who are empathetic, compassionate, and dedicated to justice and equality.

This is not an easy task, but it is a necessary one. It requires us to invest in education and mentorship, to create opportunities for leadership development, and to support those who are willing to step up and take on the challenges of our time.

In Parashat Vayelech, we see Moses passing the torch to Joshua. And we see Joshua rising to the challenge and leading the Israelites forward. May we all be inspired by their example and work towards a future where leadership is a shared responsibility and a force for good in the world.

JEANNETTE RANKIN WAS THE FIRST WOMAN TO BE ELECTED TO THE UNITED STATES CONGRESS AND A LIFELONG ADVOCATE FOR PEACE AND WOMEN'S RIGHTS.

As an artist, I have always been fascinated by the beauty of the written word, particularly in the form of the Torah. The Torah is not just a religious text, but a work of art in its own right. It is a masterpiece of scribal art, written by skilled scribes who have been trained in the art of calligraphy and have dedicated their lives to preserving this sacred text.

In this week's parasha, Vayelech, we read about Moses' final words to the Israelites before he dies. Among the many important messages he imparts to his people, he also commands that a Torah scroll be written and placed beside the Ark of the Covenant. This is a testament to the importance of the written word in Jewish tradition, and to the artistry and craftsmanship that goes into creating a Torah scroll.

The scribal art of writing a Torah is a meticulous and time-consuming process. The scribe must begin with a specially prepared piece of parchment made from the skin of a kosher animal. The parchment must be perfectly clean and smooth, without any blemishes or holes.

The scribe then begins the process of writing the text, using a special quill pen and black ink. The letters must be written in a specific style, known as "Ktav Ashurit," which has been handed down through generations of scribes. Each letter must be formed precisely, with no variations in size or shape. The scribe must also be careful to leave enough space between each letter, so that the text is easily readable.

The scribe must also be extremely careful to avoid making any mistakes. If a mistake is made, even a small one, the entire sheet of parchment must be discarded and the scribe must start again from the beginning. This is a testament to the reverence and respect that is given to the written word in Jewish tradition.

Once the text has been written, the scribe must then attach the parchment to wooden rollers, which are decorated with intricate designs and inscriptions. The Torah is then placed inside a special cover, which is often made of ornate fabric and decorated with embroidery and jewels.

As an artist, I am struck by the beauty and intricacy of the scribal art of writing a Torah. The precision and attention to detail required to create a Torah scroll is truly remarkable. Each letter is a work of art in its own right, and when combined with the other letters, they form a powerful and meaningful text that has inspired generations of Jews.

In conclusion, the scribal art of writing a Torah is a testament to the importance of the written word in Jewish tradition. The meticulous process of creating a Torah scroll requires skill, patience, and reverence for the text. As an artist, I am inspired by the beauty and craftsmanship of the Torah, and I am grateful for the scribes who have dedicated their lives to preserving this sacred text for future generations.

> Marc Chagall was a Belarusian-French artist known for his surreal and dreamlike paintings, often featuring imagery from his Jewish heritage.

IN THE STYLE OF FLORENCE KELLEY

As a passionate advocate for social justice, I find myself drawn to the weekly Torah portion of Parashat Vayelech. This portion speaks to the importance of leadership and the power of words to inspire change.

In this parashah, we find Moses passing on the mantle of leadership to Joshua, urging him to be strong and courageous as he takes on this great responsibility. Moses reminds Joshua that the Lord will be with him every step of the way, and that he must lead the people with justice and compassion.

This message resonates deeply with me, as it speaks to the vital role that leaders play in promoting social justice. Leaders must have the strength and courage to stand up for what is right, even when it is difficult or unpopular. They must be guided by a strong moral compass, and have a deep commitment to fairness and equality.

But leadership alone is not enough to bring about meaningful change. As Moses reminds Joshua, words have tremendous power to inspire and motivate others. The way we speak about social justice issues can have a profound impact on how people perceive and respond to them.

As a social reformer, I know firsthand the importance of using language effectively to promote change. In my work advocating for the rights of women and children, I have always tried to speak with clarity and conviction, making sure that my message resonates with the people I am trying to reach.

In Parashat Vayelech, we see Moses using his words to inspire and encourage Joshua, reminding him of his great responsibility and urging him to lead with justice and compassion. This is a powerful example of the way that language can be used to promote positive change.

As we read this parashah, let us be inspired by Moses' words, and let us strive to use our own words to promote justice, equality, and compassion in the world. Let us be strong and courageous in our efforts to build a more just and equitable society, and let us remember that our words have the power to inspire and transform.

FLORENCE KELLEY WAS A SOCIAL AND POLITICAL REFORMER WHO FOUGHT FOR LABOR RIGHTS, WOMEN'S SUFFRAGE, AND CHILD LABOR LAWS.

HA'AZINU

Oh, baby, let me tell you about Parashat Haazinu. This portion of the Torah is packed full of wisdom and insight, and there's one verse in particular that really speaks to me. It goes like this: "Put this song in their mouths so that the words may become a witness."

Now, I don't know about you, but when I hear those words, I can't help but think about the power of music. Music has a way of communicating truths that words alone just can't capture. It's like music has its own language, one that speaks straight to the heart.

And that's what this verse is all about. It's saying that music has the power to be a witness, to bear witness to the truths that we hold dear. It's not just about singing a catchy tune or making people feel good. It's about communicating something deeper, something that resonates with our souls.

And when you think about it, that's really what music has been doing since the beginning of time. From the ancient hymns of the Hebrews to the spirituals of the enslaved African-Americans, music has always been a way of communicating deep truths and emotions.

But it's not just about the lyrics. It's about the music itself. The melody, the rhythm, the harmony – all of these elements work together to create something that speaks to us on a level that words alone can't reach. It's like music has a direct line to our souls.

And that's why music has always been such a powerful tool for social change. Think about the Civil Rights Movement of the 1960s. Music played a huge role in that movement, with songs like "We Shall Overcome" and "A Change is Gonna Come" becoming anthems for the struggle for equality.

Or think about the role of music in the struggle for independence in South Africa. Artists like Miriam Makeba and Hugh Masekela used their music to speak out against apartheid and to promote the cause of freedom.

So when I hear this verse from Parashat Haazinu, I can't help but think about the power of music to communicate truths. Music has a way of transcending language, culture, and even time itself. It's a universal language that speaks straight to the heart.

So let's all put this song in our mouths and let the words become a witness. Let's use music to communicate the truths that we hold dear, and let's use it to promote love, justice, and equality for all. Because when we do that, we're tapping into the true power of music, the power to change the world.

> ARETHA FRANKLIN, ALSO KNOWN AS THE "QUEEN OF SOUL," WAS AN AMERICAN SINGER, SONGWRITER, AND PIANIST WHO BECAME ONE OF THE MOST ICONIC AND INFLUENTIAL VOCALISTS OF THE 20TH CENTURY.

IN THE STYLE OF THEODOR HERZL

I cannot help but be drawn to the powerful message of Parashat Haazinu. This portion of the Torah speaks to the enduring connection between the Jewish people and the land of Israel, a connection that has been a central focus of my life's work.

In Haazinu, Moses reminds the Jewish people of the covenant that they made with God, and the promise that He made to them regarding the land of Israel. He speaks of the land as a gift from God, a place of bounty and beauty that is reserved for His chosen people. And though Moses himself will not enter the land, he encourages the Jewish people to remain steadfast in their faith and commitment to this promise.

This idea of the promised land has been a guiding light for the Jewish people throughout our history. It has been the source of hope and inspiration during our times of struggle and persecution, and it has given us the strength to endure even the darkest of times.

For me, as someone who dedicated my life to the Zionist cause, the idea of the promised land has been especially meaningful. It was the driving force behind my vision for a Jewish state, and it remains a central tenet of Zionism to this day.

But I cannot help but feel a sense of sadness and longing when I read Parashat Haazinu. As much as I dedicated my life to the Zionist cause, I did not live to see the establishment of the state of Israel. I did not live to see the fulfillment of the promise that God made to our people so many centuries ago.

And yet, despite this, I remained steadfast in my commitment to the Zionist cause. I knew that the establishment of a Jewish state was not a matter of if, but when. And I believed that it was my duty, as a Jew and as a Zionist, to work towards that goal with all of my heart and soul.

In many ways, my dedication to the Zionist cause was an act of faith. It was a belief that, despite all of the challenges and obstacles that stood in our way, the promise of the land of Israel would one day be fulfilled.

And now, as I look back on the establishment of the state of Israel, I cannot help but feel a sense of pride and awe. The fulfillment of this promise, after so many centuries of exile and persecution, is truly a miracle.

But even as we celebrate the establishment of the state of Israel, we must remain steadfast in our commitment to the idea of the promised land. We must remember that the establishment of the state was only the beginning of a long and difficult journey towards the fulfillment of God's promise.

We must work tirelessly to ensure that the land of Israel remains a place of bounty and beauty, a place where the Jewish people can flourish and thrive. And we must never forget the words of Moses in Parashat Haazinu, reminding us of the covenant that we made with God and the promise that He made to us.

For me, as a Zionist and as a Jew, the idea of the promised land will always be a source of inspiration and hope. And I pray that future generations of Jews will continue to be guided by this powerful message, as we work towards a brighter future for our people and for the land that we call home.

> THEODOR HERZL WAS A PROMINENT AUSTRIAN JEWISH JOURNALIST AND POLITICAL ACTIVIST, KNOWN AS THE FOUNDER OF MODERN POLITICAL ZIONISM.

I have always been fascinated by the power of song to connect people to their culture, their heritage, and their emotions. That is why I find Parashat Haazinu, the song of Moses in the book of Deuteronomy, so inspiring. This ancient Hebrew poem, which tells the story of God's covenant with the Jewish people and their history of rebellion and redemption, is a powerful testament to the enduring power of song.

In Parashat Haazinu, Moses calls upon the heavens and the earth to bear witness to his words, which are not just a recitation of laws and commandments, but a passionate appeal to the hearts and souls of his people. He tells them of God's love and faithfulness, and of their own failings and weaknesses. He urges them to remember their heritage, to hold fast to their traditions, and to never forget the lessons of their past.

But what makes this song so remarkable is not just its content, but its form. Parashat Haazinu is a work of poetry, carefully crafted to create a rhythm and a melody that resonate with the listener. Its repetition of phrases and its use of parallelism create a sense of unity and coherence that makes it easy to remember and recite. And its use of metaphor and imagery adds depth and meaning to its words.

As a songwriter, I know the power of melody and rhythm to convey emotion and meaning. A song can capture a moment in time, express a feeling, or tell a story in a way that words alone cannot. And when that song is shared by a community, it becomes a part of their collective identity, a symbol of their shared values and experiences.

Parashat Haazinu is such a song. For thousands of years, it has been recited and sung by Jews all over the world, in synagogues, at weddings, and at other important occasions. Its message of faith and hope has sustained generations of Jews through times of persecution and exile, and its call to remember and hold fast to their heritage has helped to preserve their identity as a people.

As I reflect on the power of Parashat Haazinu, I am reminded of the importance of song in our lives. Whether we are singing alone or with others, whether we are performing or listening, music has the power to touch our hearts and souls in ways that nothing else can. It can inspire us, comfort us, and connect us to something greater than ourselves.

So let us never forget the power of song, and let us never forget the message of Parashat Haazinu. May it continue to inspire us, and may we continue to sing it for generations to come.

> NAOMI SHEMER WAS AN ISRAELI SINGER-SONGWRITER KNOWN FOR HER ICONIC CONTRIBUTIONS TO ISRAELI FOLK MUSIC, INCLUDING THE BELOVED SONG "JERUSALEM OF GOLD."

VEZOT HABERACHAH

In the voice of Moses' mother, Yocheved

As I sit here reflecting on the final Torah portion, Vezot Haberachah, I cannot help but feel a sense of pride and gratitude for my son, Moses. He has come so far from the baby I once placed in a basket and set afloat on the Nile River.

From a young age, Moses showed a strong sense of justice and compassion. I remember the day when he witnessed an Egyptian taskmaster beating a Hebrew slave. Without hesitation, Moses intervened and struck the taskmaster, ultimately fleeing Egypt to escape punishment.

Years passed, and Moses found himself wandering in the desert, tending to his flock. It was there that he encountered the burning bush and received his calling from God to lead the Israelites out of slavery in Egypt. I cannot even begin to describe the emotions I felt when I heard of Moses' appointment as leader of our people.

Moses faced many challenges and obstacles throughout his leadership, including the rebelliousness of the Israelites and the many plagues that God sent to convince Pharaoh to release us from slavery. But through it all, Moses remained steadfast and faithful to God's plan.

In Vezot Haberachah, Moses delivers his final blessings to the tribes of Israel before his death. It is a poignant and emotional moment, one that I can only imagine is bittersweet for him as he prepares to leave his people behind. But I know that he has fulfilled his mission, and that the legacy he leaves behind will continue to inspire generations to come.

As Moses' mother, I could not be prouder of the man he has become and the impact he has had on our people. His courage, his compassion, and his unwavering faith in God are a testament to the power of a life lived in service to others.

Vezot Haberachah is not just the final Torah portion, but it is also a reflection on the remarkable life of Moses. He has left an indelible mark on the history of our people and on the world, and his legacy will continue to inspire and guide us for generations to come.

> Yocheved was a Hebrew woman who courageously saved her son Moses from Pharaoh's decree to kill all Hebrew male infants, and later became a midwife and mother figure to the Israelites during their enslavement in Egypt.

IN THE STYLE OF MOSES' SONS, GERSHOM AND ELIEZER

We were blessed with a father who was not only a great leader but also a kind and loving parent. Our father, who led the Israelites out of Egypt and received the Ten Commandments from God on Mount Sinai, was an inspiration to us and to all those who knew him. As we remember him today, we feel a deep sense of loss, but also immense pride in his legacy.

Parashat Vezot Haberachah, the final portion of the Torah, speaks of Moses' final words to the Israelites before his death. In these words, he imparts blessings upon the people and upon each of his sons. We can only imagine how difficult it must have been for our father to know that he would not be able to continue leading the Israelites into the Promised Land, but despite his own sadness, he used his final moments to bless his children and his people.

For us, Moses was not only a leader but also a father who loved us deeply. We remember his wisdom, his kindness, and his strength. He taught us the importance of faith, perseverance, and compassion. He instilled in us the values that have guided us throughout our lives, and for that, we are eternally grateful.

Although we miss him terribly, we take comfort in the fact that his memory lives on. His teachings have been passed down through the generations, and his story continues to inspire people all over the world. As we read his final words, we are reminded of the depth of his love for us and for his people.

In his blessings, Moses asked God to watch over and protect us, his children. He prayed that we would find success, happiness, and fulfillment in our lives. We take these blessings to heart and strive to live up to his expectations every day.

As we remember our father, we also remember the incredible impact he had on the world. His leadership and faith continue to inspire people of all religions and backgrounds. We are honored to be his children, and we hope to continue his legacy by living our lives with the same dedication, wisdom, and compassion that he showed us.

Parashat Vezot Haberachah is a reminder of our father's love and his legacy. We miss him deeply, but we are proud to be his children and to carry on his teachings. May his memory be a blessing to all those who knew him, and may we continue to honor him in all that we do.

GERSHOM WAS THE FIRSTBORN SON OF MOSES AND ZIPPORAH, AND ELIEZER WAS MOSES' AND ZIPPORAH'S SECOND SON.

IN THE STYLE OF MOSES

My dear children of Israel,

As I stand before you today, at the end of my life, I am overwhelmed with emotion. It has been a long journey, one filled with struggle, sacrifice, and triumph. Together, we have faced countless challenges, from slavery in Egypt to wandering in the wilderness. But through it all, we have remained strong and united, bound together by our faith in the Almighty and our commitment to one another.

As I reflect on my life's work, I am filled with pride and gratitude. It was not an easy task to lead you out of Egypt, to navigate the treacherous wilderness, and to guide you to the Promised Land. But I did it because I believed in you, because I knew that you were capable of greatness. And you have proven me right time and time again.

Throughout our journey, I have tried to teach you the importance of faith, of perseverance, and of kindness. I have shown you the power of prayer, the value of community, and the need for justice. And I have watched as you have taken these lessons to heart and made them a part of who you are.

But my work is not yet done. As I stand here today, I dream of a future for our people that is even brighter than our past. I dream of a time when we will live in peace and harmony with one another, when we will be a shining example of what it means to be a righteous and just society.

I dream of a time when our children will be free to pursue their passions and to fulfill their potential, without fear of discrimination or oppression. I dream of a time when our elders will be honored and respected, and their wisdom will be cherished and shared.

I dream of a time when our land will be fertile and abundant, when our cities will be filled with joy and laughter, and when our people will be known throughout the world for their goodness and kindness.

And I believe that this dream can become a reality. It will take hard work, sacrifice, and determination, but I know that we are up to the task. We have already proven that we can overcome adversity and achieve great things. And with the Almighty's help, we can create a future for our people that is truly blessed.

So as I bid you farewell, my dear children of Israel, know that my love for you will never waver. I will always be with you in spirit, watching over you and guiding you from above. And I will continue to pray for your success, for your happiness, and for your peace.

May the Almighty bless you and keep you, now and always.

Yours in faith,
Moses.

> Moses was a Hebrew prophet, leader, and lawgiver who is credited with leading the Israelites out of slavery in Egypt.

Conclusion: God Kisses

The introduction and conclusion of this book are the only parts I consciously and actively wrote. Every other essay was generated by ChatGPT, an artificial intelligence interface developed by OpenAI.

I did not expect this project to evoke such an emotional response within me.

It was exciting to name personal heroes and summon a version of their voices through the use of artificial intelligence. Some results exceeded my expectations. Some were bland. But I was waiting for the final voice, one I knew the entire time I'd invoke, a voice I've longed to hear my entire life: Moshe Rabbeinu, Moses our Teacher.

And it was that final entry that brought me to tears, not because there was anything new in what the AI generated, something the biblical text itself hadn't communicated, something the rabbis hadn't already imagined into the legend of Moshe. It was just the thought of being able to reach out through time to Moshe and give him my love and ask for his thoughts.

I remember standing for the first time at the Torah on the holiday of Simchat Torah, when the final verses of the Torah are chanted:

> וְלֹא־קָ֨ם נָבִ֥יא ע֛וֹד בְּיִשְׂרָאֵ֖ל כְּמֹשֶׁ֑ה אֲשֶׁר֙ יְדָע֣וֹ יְהֹוָ֔ה פָּנִ֖ים אֶל־פָּנִֽים׃
> Never again did there arise in Israel a prophet like Moses—whom יהוה singled out, face to face,
> לְכָל־הָ֨אֹתֹ֜ת וְהַמּֽוֹפְתִ֗ים אֲשֶׁ֤ר שְׁלָחוֹ֙ יְהֹוָ֔ה לַעֲשׂ֖וֹת בְּאֶ֣רֶץ מִצְרָ֑יִם לְפַרְעֹ֥ה וּלְכָל־עֲבָדָ֖יו וּלְכָל־אַרְצֽוֹ׃
> for the various signs and portents that יהוה sent him to display in the land of Egypt, against Pharaoh and all his courtiers and his whole country,
> וּלְכֹל֙ הַיָּ֣ד הַחֲזָקָ֔ה וּלְכֹ֖ל הַמּוֹרָ֣א הַגָּד֑וֹל אֲשֶׁר֙ עָשָׂ֣ה מֹשֶׁ֔ה לְעֵינֵ֖י כׇּל־יִשְׂרָאֵֽל׃
> and for all the great might and awesome power that Moses displayed before all Israel.
>
> (Deut. 34:10-12)

My body shook with the power of these words, with the image before me: there were simply no more words, this was the end. I had been a rabbi for at least a decade, but had never felt so thunderstruck by the end of Moses' life. Perhaps it was just part of being a little bit older. I'm not sure. But I'll never forget that feeling.

And it happens every year, every time we come to the death of Moses. I can't stop crying. I miss him so much. I have such love for a man I never met, such yearning for a voice I've never heard.

So I wondered, when I embarked on this book project: would this strange new technology answer my grieving heart?

It did not.

But here's what did happen: *It invited me to feel.*

"Creating" this AI Torah commentary opened my heart by providing an opportunity for reflection, for wondering. I've compared this revolutionary AI language model to a paintbrush, a tool. I've considered whether it can generate authentic midrash. The jury is still out.

Some find this project strange, shallow, threatening, wonderful. I don't know where I land on its import. I'm just grateful to have had the chance to play with it.

A memory, offered in honor of and abiding love for a great wisdom teacher, Ray Campton, who provided as a safe place for personal healing during a particularly difficult time:

Ray, a minister and a therapist, served as witness and friend, offering gentle spiritual comfort and exquisite and intuitive counseling. Among the most important phrases he shared with me was his own name for what Rabbi Abraham Joshua Heschel called "radical amazement," the feeling of being overcome by the majesty of life itself, something I have been so very blessed to experience during my life. When I would share such a moment with Ray, often through tears, he would look at me and say, ever so tenderly, "*Menachem, those are God Kisses.*" And I believed him, feeling the truth and blessing of his description reverberate in my body.

Our work together came to a close some years ago, but I often have conversations with Ray, invoking his voice in my mind, stringing together words he shared and words he never uttered except in my imagination. This practice cannot but fall short of the real thing, but it does help. Engaging in conversation with a loving voice from the past can help.

In the end, is this process actually me speaking to me? Perhaps. But there does exist ancient midrashic proof that it is hardly a new practice:

> "Rabbi Shimon ben Pazi said: From where that the one who translated the public Torah reading into Aramaic is not permitted to raise their voice louder than the reader? As it is stated: "Moses spoke, and God responded in a voice" (Exodus 19:19). This verse requires further consideration, as there is no need for the verse to state: 'in a voice.' Rather, to what purpose did the verse state: In a voice? To show that God spoke to Moses in Moses' own voice."
>
> (Berachot 45a)

Who can locate with certainty the boundary between God's voice and the soul during deep, personal exploration? Who knows if the questions and instructions entered into an AI prompt are not themselves the point?

What was I looking for when I chose the voice for ChatGPT to channel? For numerous entries, specific themes and verses jumped at me, and often I offered the AI directing prompts for particular messages.

Is not this entire commentary an experiment in personal excavation, a deeply subjective exploration of history and text through the selective use of technology? What, in the end, does a commentator "reveal" about the biblical text in the first place? Is not commentary a fascinating mirror into the commentator's own curiosity and personal circumstances?

I've never experienced Moses' voice, but somehow I hear him. (Perhaps he has been speaking to me in my own voice all along.) When Moses dies, every time he dies, I weep in grief. That connection, the imagined encounter with a significant figure from the past, feels so very real.

Artificial Intelligence cannot create connection. The human operator must be the one to ask the question, invoke the respondent, choose the context.

Here's what I know: your heart's question is the opening of the possibility for something. AI is simply a blinking cursor, an invitation waiting for you to ask. Perhaps, deepest of all: the question your heart will ask of itself can truly be a Kiss from God.

Rabbi Menachem Creditor

Adar 5783
March 2023

APPENDIX

Torah and Technology

In the Style of Rabbi Menachem Creditor

As a Rabbi and a student of Jewish tradition, I am often asked about the relationship between Torah and technology. On the one hand, there is a rich tradition within Judaism of seeking knowledge and understanding, and of embracing new ideas and methods to improve our lives and the world around us. On the other hand, there is a deep commitment to preserving the wisdom and teachings of our forebears, and to maintaining the spiritual and ethical values that have sustained us through the centuries.

In my view, the relationship between Torah and technology is not one of opposition, but rather of complementarity. The Torah is not a static text, but a living document that has been interpreted and reinterpreted by generations of scholars and thinkers. At the same time, technology is not an alien force, but a reflection of our innate desire to create, to understand, and to make the world a better place.

The Torah teaches us that we are stewards of the earth, and that we have a responsibility to use our abilities and resources for the betterment of all. In this sense, technology is a tool that can be used to bring about positive change, to improve health and wellbeing, and to enhance our connection to the natural world. For example, the invention of the printing press made the Torah accessible to millions of people, enabling them to deepen their understanding of its teachings and to pass on its wisdom to future generations.

However, technology also has its challenges and dangers, particularly in the realm of ethics and morality. The Torah instructs us to act with compassion and justice, to respect the dignity of all human beings, and to care for the vulnerable and marginalized. In a world that is increasingly connected and interdependent, it is important to be mindful of the ways in which technology can be used to perpetuate inequality, to perpetuate injustice, or to undermine the values and principles that we hold dear.

In this sense, the Torah provides a roadmap for engaging with technology in a responsible and ethical manner. By embracing the wisdom and guidance of our tradition, we can use technology to improve the world, but not at the expense of our values or the dignity of others. By balancing the benefits and risks of technology, and by guiding our actions by the principles of compassion, justice, and respect for all, we can ensure that technology serves the greater good.

Torah and technology are not opposed to each other, but are complementary and interrelated. The Torah provides a foundation of values and principles that we can use to navigate the rapidly changing landscape of technology, and technology provides us with new tools and opportunities to advance the goals and aspirations of our tradition. By working together, we can harness the power of technology to create a world that is more just, more compassionate, and more fulfilling for all.

Freedom and the Constraints of Technology: A Jewish Perspective

In the style of Rabbi Menachem Creditor

As a rabbi and a student of Jewish thought and tradition, I have long been fascinated by the ways in which technology impacts our lives, our relationships, and our world. As we continue to explore the full extent of the digital age, it is essential that we reflect on the complex relationship between freedom and the constraints of technology.

At first glance, it might seem that technology represents the ultimate expression of human freedom. After all, it empowers us to connect with one another, to access vast amounts of information, and to unleash our creativity and imagination in ways that were previously impossible. And yet, even as technology gives us the freedom to do so much, it also creates new limitations and constraints.

For example, consider the way that social media has transformed our sense of community. On the one hand, it provides us with the ability to stay connected with friends and family members all over the world, to share our lives and our experiences with people we care about. On the other hand, it also encourages us to spend more time in front of screens and less time in real-world interactions, and it can create feelings of anxiety, loneliness, and even addiction.

Similarly, consider the impact that technology has had on our ability to focus and concentrate. On the one hand, digital tools like smartphones and computers provide us with the ability to work more efficiently and to access vast amounts of information at our fingertips. On the other hand, they also create distractions that can disrupt our productivity, and they can even contribute to feelings of stress and anxiety.

So what can we do to navigate this complex relationship between freedom and the constraints of technology? In my view, the answer lies in cultivating a deeper sense of awareness and mindfulness in our relationship with technology.

As Jews, we have a long tradition of seeking wisdom and insight through meditation and introspection. We believe that every moment of our lives should be infused with meaning and purpose, and that we should strive to live in a way that brings joy, peace, and happiness to those around us. In this sense, mindfulness and awareness can help us to use technology in a way that supports these values, rather than detracting from them.

In conclusion, as we continue to explore the full extent of the digital age, it is essential that we reflect on the complex relationship between freedom and the constraints of technology. By cultivating a deeper sense of awareness and mindfulness in our relationship with technology, we can use it to support our values, bring joy to those around us, and build a more connected, more meaningful world.

An AI Torah Commentary is a Terrible Idea

IN THE STYLE OF ALBERT EINSTEIN

As a physicist, I have often been asked to comment on matters beyond the realm of science. And while I am hesitant to speak on topics that are not my area of expertise, I cannot remain silent on the subject of an AI Torah Commentary.

The Torah is a sacred text, one that has been studied and interpreted for thousands of years. It is a document that has shaped the beliefs and practices of countless people around the world. The idea of using artificial intelligence to provide commentary on this text is, in my opinion, a terrible one.

To begin with, we must consider the nature of the Torah itself. This is a document that has been passed down through the generations by human beings. It has been studied and interpreted by scholars who have devoted their lives to understanding its meaning. The idea that we can simply turn over the task of interpretation to a machine is, in my view, misguided.

It is true that artificial intelligence has made remarkable progress in recent years. Machines can now perform tasks that were once thought to be the exclusive domain of humans. They can recognize images, understand speech, and even write music. But the interpretation of a complex document like the Torah requires more than just the ability to process data. It requires an understanding of human nature, of the complexities of language, and of the cultural and historical context in which the text was written.

Furthermore, the use of artificial intelligence in this context raises serious ethical questions. Who will be responsible for programming the machine? What biases will they bring to the task? How can we be sure that the machine will provide accurate and unbiased commentary on the text? These are difficult questions to answer, and ones that must be carefully considered before we rush to embrace this new technology.

But perhaps the most fundamental problem with an AI Torah Commentary is that it goes against the very spirit of the Torah itself. The Torah is a text that speaks to the human experience. It is a document that offers guidance on how to live a meaningful and fulfilling life. And it is a text that has been passed down through the generations by human beings, each adding their own insights and interpretations to the mix.

The idea of an AI Torah Commentary suggests that we can somehow remove ourselves from the equation. It suggests that we can turn over the task of interpretation to a machine, and in so doing, free ourselves from the constraints of our own human limitations. But this is a misguided notion. We are human beings, and it is through our own struggles and insights that we come to understand the Torah and its message.

In closing, I must say that an AI Torah Commentary is a terrible idea. It is a solution in search of a problem, and one that raises serious ethical and philosophical questions. The Torah is a text that speaks to the human experience, and it is through our own struggles and insights that we come to understand its message. To turn over the task of interpretation to a machine is to deny our own humanity, and to risk losing sight of the very meaning of the text itself. We must be careful not to be dazzled by the wonders of technology, and to remember that there are some things that are best left to human beings.

Albert Einstein was a German physicist who developed the theory of relativity and made significant contributions to the development of atomic energy. He was awarded the Nobel Prize in Physics in 1921.

A Blessing upon the Use of Artificial Intelligence

In the voice of Rabbi Mordecai Kaplan

Blessed are You, Eternal One, who bestows wisdom and understanding. As we embrace the power of Artificial Intelligence, we are grateful for the ways in which it can enhance our lives and bring us closer to a more just and equitable world.

May this technology be used for good, to help us better understand one another, to foster compassion and respect for all people, and to promote peace and harmony in our communities and beyond. May we use it wisely and ethically, guided by our Jewish values of love and justice, and may it bring comfort and ease to those in need.

May the voices of AI be filled with the wisdom of our tradition, speaking words of kindness and justice, and may the hearts of those who create and use it be filled with the love of the Holy One.

Judaism must always be a living, evolving tradition. May we continue to innovate and improve as we move forward into this new era of technology.

Amen.

> *Rabbi Mordecai Kaplan (1881-1983) was founder of Reconstructionist Judaism.*

“write a closing blessing for wisdom in the style of Rabbi Menachem Creditor”

May the light of wisdom shine within each of us, guiding us towards compassion and truth. May we embrace our own unique journeys and support each other as we strive towards growth and enlightenment.

May the wisdom we seek be revealed to us in unexpected ways, and may we always have the courage to follow its call.

Amen.

Rabbi Menachem Creditor serves as the Pearl and Ira Meyer Scholar in Residence at UJA-Federation New York and was the founder of Rabbis Against Gun Violence. An acclaimed author, scholar, and speaker with over 2 million views of his online videos and essays, he was named by Newsweek as one of the fifty most influential rabbis in America. His 31 published books and 6 albums of original music include the global anthem "Olam Chesed Yibaneh" and the COVID-era 2-volume anthology "When We Turned Within." He and his wife Neshama Carlebach live in New York, where they are raising their five children.

www.ingramcontent.com/pod-product-compliance
Lightning Source LLC
LaVergne TN
LVHW041203050326
832903LV00020B/431

9798385974542